or

,

A Christian Road Map for Women Traveling Alone

Jo Anne Sekowsky

Illustrated by Jean Beers
Cover illustration by Edna Haavik

AGLOW PUBLICATIONS
Edmonds, Washington

TABLE OF CONTENTS

FOREWORD

When asked to write the foreword for Jo Anne Sekowsky's book I wondered why a happily married woman should be the one chosen to write the first words about a book for the single woman.

I guess what best qualifies me for this job is that I was single for thirty-two years prior to my marriage to Dennis Bennett and so I do know something about the single life. I could have been lonely and dissatisfied as a single adult but when I finally let Him, Jesus filled my life, as He did Jo Anne's, making it full and thrilling. My Lord gave me so many adventures that I enjoyed my single life immensely. Even when the roads from time to time were bumpy, I hardly noticed the discomfort because of the joy of Jesus' presence. It can be this way for all singles when they let go and let God guide them in that perfect road plan for their life.

Then, too, we know from Scripture and experience that each of us comes into this world alone and we will leave it alone. Fortunately at the end the Christian will leave this life with Jesus holding her hand, but no earthly person can go with us. Even the married woman has times of being physically alone, for instance, when her husband's business keeps him on the job long hours, or he is required to travel out of town days or weeks at a time. Then there are those women whose husbands are home with them, but they are still alone spiritually and/or psychologically.

I truly enjoyed reading Jo Anne's book and believe it is a book to benefit all women: those actually traveling alone, those spiritually or psychologically alone, those alone temporarily or those who just need to know the problems and blessings of the single woman in order to understand and help her.

Jo Anne has the qualifications of being a high school journalism teacher and grammarian and her talent in writing is obvious. Her book teaches basics for any Christian's life. It is humorous, creatively written and illustrated, frank about the single person's problems, and has a depth to draw the reader to desire greater maturity in Christ.

I commend *A Christian Road Map for Women Traveling Alone* to you. For the single woman it's a must and, for the married woman, it will be of great benefit. The author is a petite and attractive woman, through whose quietly businesslike exterior, warmth and humor flashes as one talks with her; Jo Anne is a living testimony of what she is sharing about. Though in one way she is traveling alone, yet in another she's not, because Jesus is in the driver's seat. With a Driver and Companion like that, what adventures and excitement lie ahead on the road of life. But that's Jo Anne's story; why not read on and see?

Rita Bennett

PREFACE

To my single sisters in Christ:

You may very well ask, "Who are you to write this book?"

My credentials are simple. I am a single woman (divorced) and, though I formerly believed that the best possible life for a woman is to be happily married, I have found a deeply satisfying life, not despite the fact, but *because I am single.*

The secret of my "successful life"?

Jesus Christ!

When I began this single walk over twelve years ago, I would have made a good candidate for the lead in a soap opera — neurotic, scared, broke, nervous and desperate.

But by Jesus' love, His grace and leading, I have a different story to share today. The theme of my story reduced to a single sentence is this: Jesus is sufficient for all our wants and needs.

There is always some danger in reading a book of this nature, especially a spiritual "how-to-do it," that the reader will consider the material as proclamations of wisdom from one who has already "arrived." However, you have it on the Lord's authority that such is not my case. He has, on more than one occasion, let me know that I have a long, long way to travel on that road called Christian Perfection.

One night while listening to a speaker, I found myself thinking rather smugly, "Oh, I know that already. The Lord showed me that a long time ago."

The Lord interrupted my thoughts by saying, "When I've shown you so much, how come you've put so little of it into practice?"

Even though I trust that He was smiling as He spoke, the truth of His words was so obvious that I couldn't even come back with a "But, Lord . . ."

I pray that this book will, in effect, be a kind of sharing. With this writing I'll try to show you what the Lord is teaching me about our traveling adventures, and perhaps after you've finished reading, you'll take time to let me know what He's teaching you.

In that way we will all profit.

The Lord bless you as you read.

Jo Anne Sekowsky

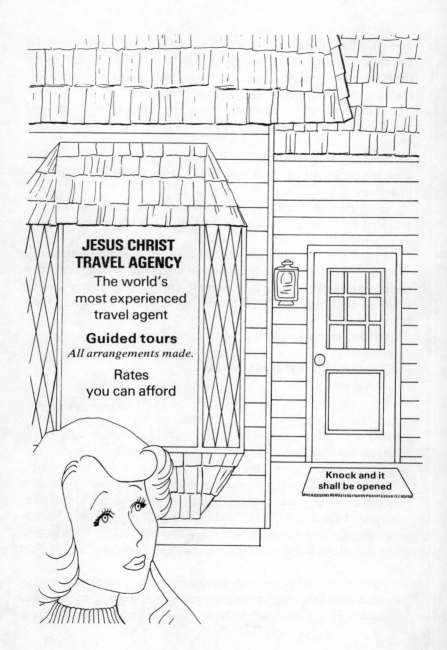

JESUS CHRIST
TRAVEL AGENCY
The world's
most experienced
travel agent

Guided tours
All arrangements made.

Rates
you can afford

Knock and it
shall be opened

12

PROLOGUE

When we set out on an earthly journey, we frequently require the services of a travel agent. Spiritually, it is no different.

Before He returned to heaven, Jesus promised, "I will never, never fail you nor forsake you." (Heb. 13:5 TLB) One of the ways He fulfills this promise is by more than adequately providing everything we need for our journey through life. I trust no one will think I am being facetious if I attribute these services to the Jesus Christ Travel Agency.

As a woman who has done a lot of solo traveling, I would like to seriously recommend Jesus as our Travel Agent. No, you won't find the Jesus Christ Travel Agency listed in the yellow pages of your telephone directory, but with a small amount of seeking you will find a branch office deep within you.

Any good travel agency provides many different kinds of services and this is particularly true of the Jesus Christ Travel Agency. But, whereas other travel agents cannot have intimate knowledge of all the places they would send us, Jesus has personally traveled every route He recommends. He knows the language and customs, the laws and regulations, even the speed limit of each place on our itinerary. He'll even advise us on how much time we should spend at each stop.

Unlike other travel agents who would plan our trip, then send us on our way alone, Jesus sends His personal guide, the Holy Spirit, to lead us through unfamiliar lands. In addition, He provides each of us with a comprehensive map of the journey — the Bible.

If we have enough faith, we can trust Jesus to plan the entire trip for us. (Just ask for the specially-prepared economy trip called The Way.)

The Jesus Christ Travel Agency has one additional feature for its customers that I know is unique. For Christians, the trip comes entirely prepaid. Jesus has already paid the whole price.

So whatever your traveling needs, come to the Jesus Christ Travel Agency. It has never had a dissatisfied customer.

I wish you a blessed trip.

The King's Library

Oh, no, I feel all alone again!

Introduction

ONE

WAY

When you listen to many single women talk, really listen with your heart, I mean, you will probably hear a variation of the theme expressed by an unmarried friend of mine when she said, "Somehow I'm always on the outside looking in. No matter how hard I try to be part of things around me, I never feel as though I completely belong to any group, not even my church."

Her feelings are typical, I believe, of those of many single women in our culture,

Like

Jean, a pretty 25-year-old divorcee:

"When I got divorced I made up my mind I wasn't going to date just to date," Jean explained. "I wanted to spare myself some of the rotten times other divorced women were experiencing on dates — you know, the idea that it's open season on divorcees.

"I tried to find a place for myself in church, but my church is very fundamental and even though people are friendly, even warm, towards me, I can't help feeling that deep down they don't really approve of me because I am divorced";

Or, like

Norma, an attractive 45-year-old widow:

When Norma's husband died, she tried to satisfy her need for a social life with church activities.

"People are delighted to have me teach a Sunday school class, sing in the choir or be on any number of committees, but when it comes to my own special niche, there really isn't one," she said. "There's a young married group, a singles' group for those under 30, a group for the older married, and one for older people in general, but I just don't fit into any of these.

"It's the same away from church. Most of my friends are couples, who were friends of my husband and mine. They don't seem to know what to do with me now that I'm widowed";

Or, like

Sue, a 28-year-old never-married young woman:

"The thing that's hardest for me to cope with," she admitted, "is the idea that there's something wrong with you if you aren't married.

"Among my own friends there are a number who are always trying to 'fix me up' with someone. It's really funny. They almost never invite me over unless they have a date for me. It's like I'm not really a person by myself. In our society, on a scale of 1-10, a never-been-married female rates a low 2."

Do any of these women sound like you? If they do, then let me say right here at the very beginning that you are living outside of God's perfect will for you.

If you feel alone, forgotten, unloved (and a whole bunch of other cliches) then probably, with a lot of help from Satan, you're walking on a road not chosen for you by your Travel Agent. In short, you haven't accepted the promises the Lord has made to you.

If, in any way, you have accepted as your lot a life that is less than filled with joy, prosperity, health and fruitfulness, then *you do not have the wonderful life God has made available to you!*

Listen to what He says:

> "Sing, Barren One, you who did not give birth; break into a song and shout aloud, you who never writhed in childbirth; for more numerous are the children of the single than the children of the married, says the Lord. Enlarge the space of your tent, and stretch out the curtains of your dwelling, do not hesitate, but lengthen your cords and make secure your tent pegs! For to the right and to the left you will expand abroad, until your descendants shall possess the nations and populate desolate cities. Fear not, for you shall not be ashamed; be not confounded, for you shall not be made to blush; you shall forget the shame of your youth, and the reproach of your widowhood you shall remember no more. For your true Husband is your Maker, the Lord of hosts is His name, and the Holy One of Israel is your redeemer; He shall be called the God of the whole earth. For the Lord has called you when you were an outcast woman and grieved in spirit, and as a woman in youth who was rejected, says your God . . . with everlasting mercy I will have compassion on you, says the Lord, your Redeemer.
>
> "Wretched one, storm-tossed and disconsolate, see . . . All your sons shall be taught by the Lord, and great shall be the peace of your children. In righteousness you shall be established; you shall be far from oppression, so be not afraid, and from terror, for it shall not come near you. They who gather to attack you do so not by Me; he who stirs up strife with you shall fall before you. Behold, it is I who created the smith who blows on the burning coals to produce a tool for his work, and I have created the devastator to destroy. No weapon that is formed against you shall prosper, and every tongue that rises against you in judgment you shall condemn. This is the heritage of the Lord's servants and their victory from Me, says the Lord."
> (Isa. 54:1-6,8,11,13-17 New Berkeley)

I get excited every time I read that passage and the rest of the chapter. Oh, I know the Lord was speaking to Israel when Isaiah spoke those words several thousand years ago, but He's speaking to you and me as well. As Christians we are spiritual

Israelites and we can claim all the promises made to those other Israelites. Yes, even today, because we serve an unchanging God, whose promises are for all times!

I also know these promises are for me and every other single woman because the Lord mentions so many of us by name:

1. the barren (both actually and spiritually)
2. the single (anyone not presently married)
3. the widow
4. the outcast woman
5. the grieved in spirit
6. the rejected
7. the wretched
8. the storm-tossed
9. the disconsolate
10. the ashamed
11. the forsaken

Surely you can find more than one description of yourself somewhere in this list. And if the Lord has put His finger on you and called you by name in these verses, it's for a good reason. Naming you was just to get your attention so you'd search for the promises He makes to you and all of us.

Look at these:

1. Our (spiritual) children shall be numerous.
2. Our descendants shall possess the nations and populate the desolate cities.
3. We shall not be ashamed.
4. We shall not be embarrassed.
5. We shall forget the shame of our youth.
6. We shall forget the reproach of our widowhood.
7. Our true Husband is our Maker.
8. The Lord is our Redeemer.
9. The Lord shall have compassion on us.
10. The Lord shall not be angry with us nor rebuke us.
11. His lovingkindness shall never leave us.
12. His covenant of peace shall never be withdrawn.

13. Our sons shall be taught by the Lord.
14. Great shall be the peace of our children.
15. We shall be established in righteousness.
16. We shall be far from oppression.
17. Terror shall not come near us.
18. Anyone who stirs up strife shall fall before us.
19. No weapon formed against us shall prosper.
20. We shall condemn every tongue against us. (We shall have justice against every courtroom lie. TLB)*

As far as I can see there is no area in my life or that of any other single woman that is not covered by these promises, no need that the Lord doesn't promise to meet.

Let's see how Christ intends to accomplish this wonderful life in and for you and me.

---

* If you still want more or there are any of these promises you don't understand, reread this chapter in several different versions of the Bible: King James, the Living Bible and the Amplified Bible, at least. You'll get a double blessing that way.

Thank you, Lord, for Your covering and protection.

Chapter 1

Traveling alone can be a frightening and bewildering experience, and many of the single women you meet reflect their fears and confusion in their life style.

There are women like Virginia, a little "mouse" of a person. Timid and soft-spoken, Virginia is almost a caricature of the women people take advantage of, and people do frequently take advantage of her.

The unmarried daughter of her family, Virginia is naturally the one expected to make a home for "Mother," with very little help from her brother and two sisters. At work, her overbearing boss blames her for most of his mistakes as well as for hers (and Virginia does make quite a few; she's easily flustered). At any social event she is the person who does the dishes and cleaning up after nearly everyone else has left.

Why does Virginia put up with being treated as a second-class citizen? Because that is the way she sees herself. Deep down inside she is terribly afraid that no one will even notice her if she doesn't doubly pay her way.

Let's look at another single woman and her fears. When Nat died, 59-year-old Florence was widowed for the second time. Always a person who preferred staying home to going out, Florence has become a recluse since Nat's death. She now stays in her house, feeling safe only with the curtains closed, and often will not answer the phone or doorbell. In the days following the funeral and the settling of Nat's "estate" she and her stepchildren quarreled bitterly and stopped seeing each other.

Now, Florence's only companion is a large, old dog of mixed heritage who acts as if he will eat anyone alive who approaches the house. Days go by with no sign of life from the house, and Florence's neighbors and friends are kept in a state of constant concern over whether she is all right or not.

Then, there is Pat, an attractive woman in her late twenties, who was married briefly as a teenager and has never married again, although she would secretly like to, very much. One of her greatest fears is that people will think she is husbandless because no one wants her, so she is all too ready to tell anyone how she would certainly never give up her freedom for a man.

Around men, she is aggressive and competitive. Recently, she joined NOW, one of the Women's Lib groups, and has avidly espoused herself to the cause of women's rights. She is frantically trying to escape her loneliness and the stigma of being unmarried by engaging in a rash of activities.

There are also many women like Bea, who has been separated from her husband Tony, an alcoholic, for over six months and who will probably soon give in to his insistence upon a divorce.

Before her separation, Bea used to daydream longingly of the "peace and quiet" that would be hers if she and her two children didn't have to live with Tony. But she has found little peace and quiet in a life that has necessitated her working at a job far below her capabilities, while "farming out" her children to a baby-sitter and facing the never-ending stream of bills that seem to come more frequently each month.

After a day's work and meeting the needs and demands of her children, Bea is usually too tired for any kind of social life. When she thinks about the future, she sees it stretching out before her bleak and lonely.

Besides their singleness, Bea, Florence and Pat have something else in common. They all believe what the world seems to be saying, "A single woman cannot live a happy and satisfying life."

And they are not willing to believe what God is saying, "I am sufficient for all your needs."

Whom are *you* going to believe?

To understand just what God is really saying to us, let's travel in another direction, a long way back to Adam and Eve in the Garden of Eden.

In the beginning, God placed Adam and Eve in a beautiful garden where they could live in complete harmony and fellowship with Him. He put only one condition on their life there: they must not eat the fruit of the tree of the knowledge of good and evil or they would die. We all know the story of how they "blew it" (cf. Gen. 3).

When Adam and Eve disobeyed God by eating the forbidden fruit, a strange thing happened: their eyes were opened and they saw that they were naked. Sin had separated them from God and through their newly-acquired knowledge, they saw themselves for what they then truly were—naked, exposed, unprotected. They tried to cover their nakedness and that evening, when God came to visit, they were afraid and hid.

It is interesting to note that as long as Adam and Eve were without sin they did not need a covering. But with their act of disobedience they opened the door to sin, and their exposed physical state was symbolic of the very real danger in which they had placed themselves.

God could justifiably have left them to take care of

themselves which, in effect, would have condemned them to physical, as well as spiritual death. But being God, with His Father's heart, He took pity on their uncovered state and provided them with a covering: clothing made of animal skins.

Now obviously, the animal skins were acquired only by the death of those animals so, in a very real sense, man's and woman's first covering was acquired through the shedding of blood. Is it too large a stretch of the imagination to believe, as some scholars do, that those skins which covered Adam and Eve's nakedness were lamb skins? And that in providing them as a covering for Adam and Eve, God prophetically acted out what He would at a later date offer to all people—the death of Jesus, the spotless Lamb, to forever cover our sins?

Although Adam and Eve were the first to sin they were not the last, by far. Men and women with their great propensity to sin have needed the Lord's covering throughout all ages, and God has stood able and ready to provide it.

Let's look at a few of the other times God has covered and still covers His children.

When the angel of death passed through Egypt, He passed over the houses whose doorposts were "covered" with the blood of a lamb (cf. Ex. 12).

When the children of Israel marched through the desert, the Lord provided them with a cloud by day and a pillar of fire by night. In addition to leading them and giving them light, the cloud protected "covered" them from the fierce desert heat by day; the pillar of fire, from the desert cold at night (cf. Ex. 13-21).

In Psalm 91, we have the beautiful picture of the Lord as a great bird, covering His chicks with His feathers and His wings.

What was only a foreshadowing in the Old Testament was made a reality with the death of Jesus upon the cross. Just as His shed blood becomes a covering for all the confessed sins of the Christian, it also provides a very real covering or protection for the Christian's whole life.

Women, do you realize what this means? It means that if we have accepted Jesus as Savior and Lord, then by His blood we are hidden in Him, clothed with His righteousness, protected and defended, pardoned and forgiven. All this is conveyed by the different meanings of the word *covering* in the Bible, and this covering is sufficient for all our needs, wherever our travels may take us.

However, before we can make these promises work in our lives, there is one catch. I'm not going to tell you that it's a little catch. As a matter of fact it's a very difficult one for many people to put into practice in their lives.

Here it is:

While the covering provided by the blood of Jesus for the eternal salvation of our souls is complete (independent of conduct), experientially *the Lord will cover only as much of us and our life as we give Him.*

Let me explain with an illustration. One rainy afternoon, not wanting to get my hair wet, I covered my head with a plastic rain bonnet.

Now the rain bonnet was plenty big for my head and my hair. The only problem was that I didn't get all my hair under it. When I got to work, I took off the bonnet and, of course, the hair under the covering was perfectly dry; the part that was exposed was just as wet as if I hadn't worn the rain bonnet at all. In other words, part of my hair got wet because it wasn't covered.

Our lives are like my hair that day. The part we give to the Lord He covers; the part we hold back remains exposed.

In order to be completely protected we must not knowingly sin, and if we do, we must repent. In addition, we must give the Lord every area of our life—our job, our leisure time, our children, our friends, our fears, our singleness (yes, even that), giving them to Him to do with as He pleases.

Oh!

Yes, oh, indeed, Of course, total commitment, giving the

Lord everything, is a difficult road and not too well traveled. However, our Travel Agent recommends it because it is the safest one to take. The Lord is above all our Father, and He is very patient with His children. If we can't make a complete commitment in some area for now, He'll settle for our just being willing to do so. Maybe we aren't even willing yet. Well, then, He'll settle for the first step, our being willing to be made willing.

You see, our Father loves us so terribly much that for this present time of grace He'll accept any part of us we're willing to give Him, and He'll bless that little portion in abundance.

Let's take a quick look at a real problem faced by many single women, fear of living alone. Now, if you ask a woman exactly what it is she fears, she may not be able to tell you. Often it isn't anything definite, more like something a girl I worked with expressed, "Oh, I don't know what it is I'm scared of. It's sort of a combination of robbers and of things that go bump in the night, and, oh, of just being alone."

The real problem, however, as I see it is not so much what we're afraid of, *but where our trust is.* If we're depending on locks, a dog, an alarm system or the police to protect us, we may well have reason to fear. Of course, we should take reasonable care. A dog is a good precaution; locks and alarms are great and the police will do their best, but in this day and age the job can be too much for them.

The Lord is the only one who can keep us and our possessions safe.

I know what I'm talking about. I've taken a good look at my house and there is no way to keep out anyone or anything that's determined to get in. Even my ferocious-sounding dog trembles and cowers in fear if someone calls her at her bluff, and where I live police protection is sparse.

I have to trust the Lord. Everyday I ask Jesus' protection over my household, and although most of my neighbors had had some of their possessions "liberated," I've never had any trouble in the nine years I've lived here. My family and possessions have remained secure because we are covered (protected) by the blood of Jesus.

This covering of the Lord is available to all Christians any time we need it and that includes single women: all the Virginias, the Florences, the Pats and the Beas and, yes, even you.

Have you ever wondered just exactly what this beautiful covering of the Lord is? I found this description of it in Song of Solomon 2:4, "He brought me to the banqueting house, and *his banner over me was love.*"

One version of the Bible translates "banner" as "canopy" and the Amplified Bible expands the thought, "For love waved as a protecting and comforting banner over my head when I was near him."

Christians, even we who are single wayfarers, by our request and commitment are protected by the Lord's covering—a covering of His perfect love.

CAUTION

ROAD CONSTRUCTION AHEAD

The boss wants this road made straight and level.
You know, "Make straight the paths."

Chapter 2

CAUTION:

GOD AT

WORK

Jeannie is an attractive junior in college who grew up in a home with conventional ideas concerning sex. She is engaged to a young instructor at the college she attends and, as do many of the engaged couples in their crowd, Jeannie and Harold "sleep" together. Lately, Jeannie has been feeling guilty about their relationship, but she tells herself that this is due to her middle-class upbringing and is, after all, a small price to pay for sexual freedom. She is now having counseling sessions with a psychologist, who is helping "free" her from her guilt.

Sandy, a stenographer in a business office, has been married twice. Widowed at 19, she quickly married the first man she dated after her husband's death. This marriage turned out to be a tragic mistake; most of the time the young man preferred his homosexual friends to her. After nine years of marriage and two children, Sandy divorced him for her own economic protection, when he ran out on her, leaving her with a long string of bills to pay.

Now thirty, Sandy finds herself in love with Bill, a man her age who would like to marry her but doesn't want her children. More and more frequently, Sandy is considering the idea of leaving the children with her parents and marrying Bill.

"After all," she reasons, "fate or something has dealt me two lousy hands already. I deserve any happiness I can get."

Marti, a 25-year-old bookkeeper, was devoted to her father before his death. When he died she almost had a nervous breakdown, till a friend showed her how to "hear" from her father by using a ouija board. Along with the ouija board, Marti has become interested in horoscopes and astrology and she spends much of her spare time pouring over books on the occult. Lately she has become increasingly fascinated with the subject of reincarnation.

These three women have one very basic trait in common. They have all fallen victim to one of Satan's most potent lures and are busily speeding down that wide and pleasant highway, pursuing the old, old belief that a person can live in her own "liberated" way and not suffer the consequences.

Desire for freedom has become the keynote of our generation. It comes wearing many different faces: freedom for laborers from management's "tyranny," freedom for students from the "abuses" of the educational system, freedom for children from parental "restrictions," freedom for homosexuals from social "ostracism," freedom for everyone to do his own thing.

You already know that women have not remained immune to this freedom binge; Women's Lib is intoxicating women in many countries around the world. But did you know that God has been concerned with liberating women ever since Adam and Eve sinned? Because He is a loving Father, God points out the way to true freedom for women.

God's answer to the Women's Liberation movement is called "headship."

Before some of you react strongly to the word "headship,"

hear me out.

Christianity contains many paradoxes that do not make sense to the world's way of thinking:

In order to live, we must die.

In order to receive, we must first give.

In order to have authority, we must first be under authority.

Is it strange then that, in order to be free, we must first come under submission?

What do *you* think of when you hear the word "headship"? If your mind conjures up a picture of bondage, even slavery, that is because you have listened to the world's ideas rather than God's. I know this picture is exactly the opposite of what headship actually is because I have had the experience to prove it.

The application of headship in my life has been one of the most liberating experiences I have ever known. I know it can prove the same in your life because it is not my idea, not man's, but God's, and He wants His children to be free.

"You've got to be out of your tree," I can almost hear some women thinking. "Headship is an idea out of the Dark Ages, one perpetuated by men to keep women in suppression."

"Today we know that men and women are equal."

"You're not going to catch me submitting to some fool man. That's the way to slavery!"

If you think along these lines, you are revealing something very important about yourself. If "headship," "submission," or "obedience" are words that make you come out fighting, what you are actually saying is that you reject God's evaluation of you and *all* women!

Let's take a look at how God evaluates women. Scripture says:

> "And it was not Adam who was deceived, but [the] woman who was deceived and deluded and fell into transgression."
> (I Tim. 2:14 Amp.)

"For of this sort [unregenerate men] are they which creep
into houses and lead captive silly women . . ." (II Tim. 3:6)

Many women have interpreted this realistic estimation of
them as proof that God really doesn't love women. Can you
believe this in light of Jesus' life on earth?

The Lord has a very special love for women. He has shared
some of His choicest favors with us in a way He never has with
men.

Consider:

It is to woman that He has entrusted perhaps His greatest
gift, the sharing of creation itself: the ability to conceive and
nourish life in and with her own body. The ultimate proof of
this came when He chose Mary to conceive, through the Holy
Ghost, the human Jesus.

It was also to a woman, Mary Magdalene, that Jesus first
appeared after His resurrection; it was to still a third Mary,
the sister of Lazarus, that God gave the discernment to see
Jesus' purpose, as evidenced when she anointed His feet with
the costly perfume. No man, not even the disciples, was given
that understanding.

God loves women so much that He has filled them with a
great hunger for fellowship and knowledge of Him. He has
given them a spiritual openness that makes it easier for them
to accept Jesus than it is for most men.

But loving someone doesn't mean you aren't conscious of
her faults, does it? Does a parent love her children any less
because they aren't perfect?

Because we see traits in our children that we don't like
doesn't change our real love for them. Because they are
sometimes selfish, argumentive, dishonest, even rebellious on
occasion, doesn't alter a mother's love. True, we occasionally
may have trouble liking them, but our basic love remains
unchanged. We continue to feed, clothe and house them. We
continue to work for and desire the best for them (that's what
love is all about).

God's love is much more perfect than ours and, just as we

34

are not blind to our children's faults, neither is God blind to ours. He knows that from Eve to her Twentieth-Century sister, we are easily deceived by Satan and his cohorts.

Can you seriously dispute God's evaluation? All the evidence is in His favor. Look at the number of cults that were founded by women—Christian Science, Technocracy and Unity, to name a few. Who is almost always the first to be misled by Satan, when he appears as an angel of light? Who are the prime adherents of astrology? Who is it that wants to have their palms and tea leaves read? Who fills the coffers of the self-appointed evangelists that hit town? Who frequents seances and sees questionable manifestations the most?

Women, of course!

And why do they make these mistakes? Because, when they are not under headship, they are easily deceived just as God says they are. Unfortunately, deception is not the end of the road. God further says that because women are deceived they fall into transgression (cf. I Tim. 2:14) and are led captive (cf. II Tim. 3:6).

Now, if *you* were a loving God and *you* wanted to protect this woman you had on your hands, what would *you* do?

I believe you would do exactly what God has done. He has developed a plan whereby all women can be protected, guided and cherished. He puts them in submission to men because men are usually by nature much more skeptical and objective about spiritual matters. No, I did not say that *every* woman is subject to *every* man. But just as a married woman finds her headship in her husband (cf. I Cor. 11:3b), so each single woman can find hers in specific relationships that are approved by God.

I don't believe that God ever meant for women to travel alone at the mercy of Satan and a cold, uncaring world. I say this because whether it is just a jaunt or a major excursion the Bible provides evidence that women, no matter what their state, were supposed to be cared for. (Notice I said, "supposed to.") In biblical days an unmarried daughter lived with her

35

family (cf. Gen. 24); the divorced wife often returned to her father's family (cf. Lev. 22:13); the young widow either married her husband's nearest relative (cf. Ruth 4:5) or returned to her family (cf. Ruth 1:8); older widows were supposed to be cared for by their families (cf. I Tim. 5:16); if the widow was truly destitute, then and only then, was the Church to provide for her (cf. I Tim. 5:16).

God sums up His concern for all the truly desolate when He declares that the treatment of the widow and the orphan is one of the tests of true religion (cf. Jam. 1:27). Today, I believe God would also include many others in that category, including the divorced and unmarried.

No, I am not advocating a complete return to ancient customs. Our present sociological structure is too far removed from the biblical pattern for it to be practical today. In some cases, for instance, the return of unsubmitted adult children to their parents' home could create more chaos and confusion than either party could stand, perhaps leading to a further alienation of the generations. Today it is entirely possible for a young woman to live away from home and still be submitted to her parents' counsel and guidance. Here I am speaking of normal family relationships. These principles cannot always be applied where mentally ill or alcoholic parents are involved.

Even though we cannot practice headship in exactly the same manner as the Israelites and early Christians did, the principle still stands: that women are easily deceived and each needs the counsel, guidance and protection of one or several men in many areas of her life.

Can you see that headship is closely related to God's covering? Of course, we are *all* under God's headship but that headship is usually administered through people here on earth. It is sometimes *only* through means of headship that God's covering is operative.

Exactly how does headship work? Let me give you a few principles to follow. For a married woman, headship is not that complicated—the head of the married woman is her husband (cf. Eph. 5:23).

But where does the single woman find her headship? She has two possibilities, neither of them mutally exclusive. First, her father or a male relative may be her "head," and secondly, her church, as represented by the minister or elders.

Many ministers express the feeling today that the Lord is providing families in the church who will "adopt" those singles who have no other families, giving them the companionship and guidance they need, fulfilling the promise made in Psalm 68:6, "God setteth the solitary in families."

In some churches, for instance, single people have been incorporated into small, intimate prayer groups. Each prayer group is small enough to provide a personal sharing relationship among its members that makes it, in reality, a family.

Recently, one such group was immediately able to rally around and give support to a young widow who lost her six-year-old son and was injured in an automobile accident. Under the leadership of its elder, the group lovingly took over the role of husband and family to this young woman, providing for everything she needed, even to the taking care of the funeral arrangements.

Ask the Lord to show you the person or persons who are to provide headship for you. When you receive some direction, discuss it with that person to see if he is willing to be your "head." If he isn't, then you need to do some more praying.

Don't be too surprised if the Lord leads you back to your family, as He did Marianne. Marianne was a young art student, who had turned down her father's offer to study advanced art on the West Coast and, instead, left her family to pursue an art career far from home. In New York City she soon tired of her bohemian life in a cold water flat but, embarrassed by her lack of success, she was reluctant to come home. Only after she became a Christian, did she recognize the Lord's leading to return home. Following an apologetic and happy reunion with her family, Marianne has accepted her father as her "head" and now lives in an apartment near her family. She consults her father on all important matters, recognizing that God gives her sound direction through him.

We as a generation may have rejected God's concept of family relationships, but God has not changed His mind.

Let me give you another example. Elders working with the Jesus people reported some cases of apparent failure in successfully ridding their converts of drug addiction. Many times the people wanted to be delivered; prayers were said for their deliverance from the addiction, but it persisted.

Eva was typical of many of these former flower children. Turned on to drugs in the late sixties, she found Jesus in early 1970. But try as she would, she could not entirely shake off her drug habit. Only after following the counsel of her elders, who had been directed by God to send her back to her family to live under the headship-relationship was Eva finally able to overcome the addiction.

As a single woman, don't be too concerned if your parents aren't Christians. If you will be submitted to them, as to Christ, (except in cases where they would require something of you that is obviously contrary to God's way, such as immorality or denial of your faith) your act of will, will enable the Lord to work through them. It may even be that your loving submission is the very thing that will in time lead them to Jesus.

Most single women, of course, will not be led to return to their parents' home. Barbara, a middle-aged widow, has placed herself in submission to a couple in her church. Fred, the husband, is an elder and he and his wife Terri frequently work with Barbara in church activities. They have made Barbara a real member of their family, including her in on all important family occasions and holidays.

In selecting a head, you might consider a few practical rules of thumb:

1. Never, never select a person that you are in any way

physically attracted to. Be extremely honest with yourself in this matter. That great big case of "spiritual love" you feel for a person can, in a very short time, easily turn into human love with all its accompanying complications and problems.

2. If the person you select is a married elder of the church, discuss your need with both him and his wife before he accepts the responsibility. If the wife is at all reluctant, then he is not the right elder for you. His first responsibility is to his own wife and family, not to you, no matter how great your need.

3. Once having selected a head to advise you, follow his advice, even when it goes against what you want to do. If you only want to follow your own wishes, you have not yet developed a submissive and trusting attitude.

Every woman's relationship with the person or persons the Lord places over her will be different. If the person is your father or a male relative, your relationship will probably be much closer and all-inclusive and one in which you would naturally seek advice in many more aspects of your life than you would if he were unrelated.

If the person is your minister or an elder in your church, he may be someone to whom you will go only when you have a *serious* problem.

The answers to so many of our questions are in the Bible if only we will search through it and, once having found the answers, accept them and put them into practice. The Holy Spirit will also give guidance in all avenues of our lives but will never contradict revelation of God's will in the Bible.

In the past seven years since my Baptism in the Holy Spirit I can only remember a few times, after praying and searching the Scriptures, that I have remained unsure of what action to take: once when I was having some trouble with one of my daughters and another time when I couldn't decide if I should take part in a teachers' strike.

I believe I am also under the headship of my church, and I submit to its teachings and regulations and follow its doctrines, including those with which some other churches may not agree (such as mode of baptism, marriage, remarriage and divorce). Should I ever come to the point where I cannot do this in good conscience then I believe it will be time to ask the Lord to lead me to a church whose doctrine and teachings I can accept.

I said before that coming under headship has been a liberating experience for me. Do you begin to see what I mean?

As a divorcee with two children, no living parents or male relatives, I automatically fall under the headship of my church and my pastor and elders. Knowing what the Bible, my church and pastor teach, I am freed from making the personal decisions on so many problems that seem to plague people, including Christians, today.

I do not have to spend countless hours and much energy trying to determine the right course to follow because my path is laid out before me. I do not have to suffer the torment of conscience and guilt over mistakes unwittingly made. For example, when the subject of re-baptism was causing conflict in some charismatic circles, I simply followed the teachings of my church. When the issue of abortion was put on the state ballot, had I not already known how to vote, I could have talked the issue over with one of my priests. When I cannot hear that inner voice of God speaking to me directly because of the world's tumult or my own emotional conflicts, God speaks through the voice of my elders as long as they are submitted to His word, in a way I can understand.

In short, headship has given me exactly what the Lord implies that it will give me—a kind of leading that keeps me from falling into transgressions and becoming a captive.

Let me ask you a question. Who has the greater inner freedom and security — a child who knows where she is allowed to go or one whose boundaries are never definitely fixed and who is even allowed to determine her own limits?

Of course, it is the child who is "restricted" by a loving

parent or guardian. I want to be as that child, restricted within the infinite bounds of God's protective love, yet free to explore the priceless treasure of that love. I want to be as that child, not in her immaturity and *childish* ways but in her child-like simplicity and trust in the strength and tenderness of the Father. Herein lies the way to true liberation.

**Sometimes I think I'd make more progress
if I could just move ahead of Him.**

Chapter 3

MERGING TRAFFIC

Frances is secretary to two men who are brothers in a small family business. Although their father technically owns the business, the sons are being given increasing responsibility each year.

However, there is a serious problem. The two brothers are temperamentally very different and the difference is reflected in the way they expect Frances to work. If she pleases one of them she is almost certain to annoy the other.

To top things off, both brothers are exceedingly jealous of one another.

Caught in the middle of their family problem, Frances finds herself growing tense and nervous and frequently is unable to sleep at night, even after taking doctor-prescribed tranquilizers.

One afternoon after a particularly trying work day Frances told her problem to the men's father and asked him to do something about her situation. Instead of sympathizing with her, the man became defensive about his sons and told

Frances that, if she wanted to keep her job, she would have to learn to work with the two men.

He told his sons about Frances' visit and for once they agreed about something. They were both angry with her!

Frances' job situation seems to grow steadily worse. She finds herself dreading to go to work, and yet she is reluctant to quit at this point because she most certainly will receive poor references if she does.

Obviously, Frances is being unfairly treated on her job. But what can she do about it without getting fired? Particularly, what can she, as a Christian woman, do about it?

Well, before we put our limited minds to the task of solving Frances' problem, let's see if we can figure out what the Lord would have her do.

Once having ordained headship as a liberating force in a woman's Christian walk, the Lord did not sit back and rest, as well He might have. He knew women (and men, too) would be traveling into many situations where regular "headship" would not necessarily function. And knowing His creation intimately, He also knew that, left to their own devices, men and women far too often would take the wrong turn.

His solution to this problem was to extend the *principle* of headship into other areas. Let's call this the Christian "rules-of-the-road."

The Bible very clearly tells us that we are to be submissive to:

1. Our parents. "Children, obey your parents in the Lord: for this is right. Honor thy father and mother (which is the first commandment with promise;) that it may be well with thee, and thou mayest live long on earth." (Eph. 6:1-3)

2. Our ministers. "Obey your spiritual leaders and be willing to do what they say. For their work is to watch over your souls, and God will judge them on how well they do this." (Heb. 13:17 TLB)

3. Our government. "Submit yourselves to every ordinance of man for the Lord's sake: whether it be to king, as

supreme: or unto governors, as unto them that are sent by him for the punishment of evildoers and for the praise of them that do well, for so is the will of God . . ." (I Pet. 2:13-15)

4. Our employers. "Servants, be subject to your masters with all fear: not only to the good and gentle, but also to the froward [perverse]. For this is thankworthy, if a man for conscience toward God endure grief, suffering wrongfully." (I Pet. 2:18-19)

5. Our delegated authorities (teachers, elders etc.) "But remember this, that if a father dies and leaves great wealth for his little son, that child is not much better off than a slave until he grows up, even though he actually owns everything his father had. He has to do what his guardians and managers tell him to do until he reaches whatever age his father sets." (Gal. 4:1-2 TLB)

The theme of being under authority is a dominant one in the Bible. Jesus Himself said He did only what the Father told Him to do.

When the centurion came, asking that his servant be healed, he told Jesus it was not even necessary for Him to come to his house.

> " 'For,' he said, 'I also am a man set under authority, having under me soldiers, and I say unto one, Go, and he goeth: and to another, Come, and he cometh: and my servant, Do this; and he doeth it.'
> "When Jesus heard these things He marveled at him and turned him about, and said unto the people that followed Him, I say unto you, I have not found so great faith, no not in Israel." (Luke 7:8-9)

The centurion said he *also* was a man under authority, meaning he recognized that Jesus was under authority. And Jesus praised him for his faith [his understanding].

Joseph in the Old Testament is another example of a man under authority. He was second only to Pharoah in the whole land. As long as he expressed Pharoah's wishes, everyone had to obey him. But had he come out from under that authority, he would have lost his position and probably his life as well.

We are also under authority, under the direct authority of Jesus: He frequently speaks to us directly. He also speaks to us indirectly through these authorities He places over us.

"But what if . . .?" I can mentally hear questions in so many minds.

"What if my boss takes advantage of me?"

"What do I do if I find myself caught in the middle between two authorities in my life?"

"What if I am asked to do something that is against my conscience?"

How do the rules-of-the-road work in situations like these?

Before we try to answer these questions, let's get back to Frances. You remember we left her in a pretty uncomfortable position with her job more or less in jeopardy. Let's see how the rules-of-the-road apply in her situation.

The problem of determining what Frances should do is complicated by two facts. In one sense Frances has already done too much. In another, she has not done enough.

First, let's look at what Frances should not have done.

Frances' biggest mistake was in not following the rules-of-the-road. Since she was in the employ of the two sons she should never have gone "over their heads." This is one of the most fundamental rules-of-the-road. If Frances felt she must do something about her situation she should have asked to meet with the two brothers and explained to them that she was willing to do whatever they decided jointly and tried to make them understand the difficulty of trying to follow conflicting instructions.

This kind of approach might or might not have borne fruit, but the Bible teaches the principle that if we have difficulty with someone we must first go to that person (cf. Matt. 18:15).

Even this idea is attempting to solve on a human level what very well may be a spiritual problem. What Frances needs most of all to do is to ask the Lord what He is trying to teach her in this situation and assure Him that she is willing to learn it. Rest assured that she will have to learn what the Lord wants her to learn at some point; if not on this job, then on another one or in some other area of her life.

Next, she must offer the whole situation to God, asking Him to bring good out of it (cf. Rom. 8:28). This will clear the way for the Lord to work. If she trusts Him, He will in time direct her in what she should do, perhaps even leading her to a new, more satisfying job.

What does an employee do when her boss takes advantage of her? Paul Tournier, Swiss Christian psychiatrist, tells in one of his books of a middle-aged worker who was caught in an intolerable work situation. His employer was an unhappy man who took out his frustrations on his employees. Finding another job in his line of work was not open to the employee and beginning anew in some other career at his age seemed equally impossible. Life was becoming unbearable. In his anguish, the man gave the problem to the Lord.

A short time later, the employer began singling out this man to talk to. Gradually as the two men grew to know one another, the employer revealed the ugly home life that made him so difficult a person to work for. The employee found himself filled with compassion for his employer, and his whole attitude changed. In time, he found himself enjoying both his job and his new friendship with his employer.

But what about the person who is caught between two conflicting authorities? What should she do?

Nineteen-year-old Grace lives at home with her parents and works in a stenographers' pool with a large corporation. Each month all the stenographers are required to work overtime for two or three evenings. They are always paid for the extra hours, but Grace's father feels she should not be required to work overtime. Each month the situation around Grace's home becomes very tense.

There should be no real conflict in a situation like that which Grace is involved in. As long as she is paid by her

47

employer and not asked to do anything out of order, she is under his authority at work and her parents' authority at home.

In different areas of our lives we may very well have different authorities. Just as our parents' headship ends when we enter the world of work, so we most likely do not go to our pastor for financial advice or take legal or medical problems to our teacher.

Today, the subject of personal conscience is much in the news. All of us may very well be faced with an order from a parent, employer or government that we feel we cannot, in good conscience, follow, as were Peter and the Apostles, as recorded in Acts 5:29 and Daniel, in Daniel 3:18.

What do we as Christian women do?

There are several approaches we can take when faced with this problem. First, we must determine whether the issue is truly one of conscience or is personal convenience at stake here, too?

When the problem of a teachers' strike loomed up in my school district a few years ago, I spent several painful weeks trying to sort out my feelings. If I decided not to strike, was it because I believed the strike to be wrong, or were some of my feelings based on fear of retaliation from the administration? Was the fact that I would lose several days' pay influencing my decision?

On the other hand, if I decided to strike, was it because I believed in the issue at stake enough to risk my job, or was I afraid of losing the friendship of and good working relationships with other teachers? Fortunately, my "head" was able to help me make a decision I could live with in good conscience.

We can also look for some alternate routes to follow. Say, for instance, as happened to an acquaintance of mine, that your employer wanted you to claim additional expense account items so he could take them off his taxes. Of course, as a Christian you cannot comply. However, you may discern that your employer's real motive is not to be dishonest, but rather to save money. Perhaps you can come up with some idea that will do exactly this, if not on his taxes, then on some small or big economies around the office.

Then you can tell him that, while you are unable to do as he asks, you do have some other ideas for saving money. Obviously, you must be careful not to sound condescending when you make your refusal.

Of course, there will be times when you will be asked to do something that is against your conscience and for which there is no alternative route. In refusing to obey, however, a person must face the very real risk of incurring displeasure and of punishment. Any refusal must be made with the attitude either implied or stated that "while I cannot do as you ask, I respect your right to punish me" (in the case of a parent or an agency of the government) or "your right to dismiss me" (in the case of an employer). If I cannot accept the leadership of my employer I am far better off looking for another job than remaining in one which creates bitterness in me.

God specializes in bringing good out of the impossible situations that we give to Him. But He will rarely work as long as we are struggling to solve them ourselves. If we follow the world's way of leaving God out of our problem-solving, we will only set up roadblocks to successful resolution.

Today, we live in an age when men and women are rebelling against virtually every established authority and law. As a high school teacher I have often felt surrounded by this spirit of rebellion, and something deep within me is offended when a student refuses to respect me or the classroom regulations.

Also as a Christian I am conscious of the delegated authority of my position. Up to a few years ago, the courts recognized it, too. *In loco parentis* meant that the schools acted in the parents' stead during the hours a student was in school, including administering punishment when it was called for. But recent court decisions have, to a large measure, stripped the schools of this position.

Nevertheless, I believe that God places each student in my classes because there is something He wants that particular student to learn. If a student refuses to learn what the Lord would teach him at school, then I feel sorry for him because I know he is going to have to learn that lesson somewhere else—at his job, in his marriage, or as a parent—but somewhere.

It is sad to work in places where employees literally spend all their coffee breaks and lunch hours griping about working conditions and the boss' latest "ultimatum." How much more relaxed and conscience-free is the worker who comes to the job with the attitude of "I've been hired to do a job, and I'll do it to the best of my ability."

As in headship, God's rules-of-the-road are another aspect of His liberating love for us. They provide us with a traffic pattern that enables us to drive with competence and ease, assured of a safe and enjoyable trip.

Lord, are You SURE this is the best way to go?

Chapter 4

EXPRESSWAY

Jesus said, "Lo, I am with you always, even unto the ends of the earth," and the Psalmist proclaimed, "Yea, though I walk through the valley of the shadow of death, I will fear no evil; for thou art with me . . ."

Lovely words, beautiful promises, but are they true? Unusual is the single woman who has not more than once wondered if God's grace is really sufficient to sustain her in all things. Or, even more importantly, will He always provide that grace exactly when she needs it? Will His presence be there strongly enough to enable her to travel through the really dark places?

Let's face it—as single women we are probably more keenly aware of a sense of isolation than anyone else. There have been too many times in most of our lives when we have felt completely alone, when there didn't seem to be even one person who cared. Is it going to be that way with Jesus, too?

Oh, it's fine to know intellectually that He is really there, that Jesus lives in our hearts, but that intellectual knowledge is not always enough. What we need to know is whether or not we will be able to feel or experience His presence. Will He honestly sustain, support and uplift us when we need Him most? Can He truly give us joy in times of personal sorrow?

The answer to all these questions is an unequivocal yes.

Let's get down to the real nitty-gritty. Let's start with death, because that's where the big test lies—that's the point where we know that no human consolation, no strength of character, no old-fashioned will power is likely to be sufficient to do the job we need done.

When my father died, I was a Christian but not yet baptized in the Holy Spirit. At the funeral, just when the going got rough, I suddenly experienced the comfort of the Lord.

I was very grateful for this sense of His presence and also surprised, I must admit, because I didn't know Him well enough then to trust completely in His promises. You might say that the Lord's presence came as a kind of emotional dividend. I had not expected it nor counted on it, yet it was very nice to know it could be depended on.

Eight years later, when my mother died, I knew the Lord much more intimately through the Baptism in the Holy Spirit. I knew I could trust Him to do what His Word promised and, of course, He didn't let me down.

Two years previously we had learned that my mother had leukemia. The doctors had expected her to die then, but she pulled through the initial attack in such a miraculous way that we believed she was completely healed of the disease.

Then one day a friend called me at work to say that she had just taken my mother to the hospital for a very bad inner ear infection. As we talked on the phone the peace of the Lord absolutely overwhelmed me and I found myself "knowing" that this was no temporary trip to the hospital. *Mother was going to die!*

I continued "knowing" this for the next two weeks during all the times the doctor minimized my mother's illness, even when he told me at one point that I would be able to take Mother home the next week.

Of course, I wavered in my certainty. I had no way of being sure whether God had actually given me this knowledge or whether I was just imagining it; especially in light of the doctor's opinion and the fact that many of our friends believed they had received "prophecy" saying Mother was going to be healed. I was frequently confused by the contradictions and might have passed off my knowledge if the Lord's presence had not been so real and continuous to me during this whole time. Jesus was literally with me every minute during those two weeks.

There is one place while I was driving along the road to my house, where His presence with me was so strong I could have told you the exact place He occupied in my car. I still occasionally get an emotional jolt whenever I pass that spot.

A time which could have been emotionally crippling and despairing was turned into a time of triumph and joy by the Lord. (We even sang and held prayer meetings at Mother's bedside.)

In addition to giving me His presence, the Lord completely ordered my days during those weeks. Although I was working and had two young daughters at home, there was almost no strain and very little confusion.

The Lord's final gift to me the night Mother died was to allow me to be with her at the end. I had just put on my coat and was leaving for the night, when Mother suddenly opened her eyes (she had been in a coma for several days), so I decided to stay a little longer. Within half an hour she died and I went home to my family with the sure knowledge that she was with the Lord.

I continue to miss my mother, but because of the Lord's grace to me I have never grieved over her death.

I have seen this same sustaining power exhibited in a young wife who, at her husband's funeral, walked down the aisle of the church, comforting the other mourners.

"Don't cry," she told them radiantly, "He's with Jesus now."

It is this same comforting presence that enabled another friend to lead her friends in the singing of the family's favorite hymn at the graveside as they buried her 14-year-old son.

Is this a very special grace that is reserved only for those "big" situations?

I don't think so. I felt the same loving presence the morning my old, sick tomcat died.

Spanky McFarland had, more or less, moved in on us uninvited. Completely tailless, with very short legs, Spanky looked more like a fur-covered tank than a cat and people frequently asked me, "What is it?"

Spanky was the kind of cat who had an awful lot to say about everything as he slowly moved around the house, not in a complaining sort of way, but just to keep up his end of the conversation.

When Spanky caught pneumonia he seemed to have no resistance at all, and it was evident he wouldn't live long. As I left for school one morning knowing I probably wouldn't see Spanky alive again, I felt like crying for my old "friend."

Then suddenly, Jesus was there and as I experienced that same comforting presence, my sorrow was relieved. I truly knew that He, "whose eye is on the sparrow," also cared for sick cats and all other living creatures. I was able to go to work then knowing that Spanky was in the best of hands.

Jesus' presence is available to me and to you, too, any time we need Him.

Let me tell you another story. One morning I arrived at work very upset. When I had left home a few minutes before, my older daughter was in tears. She was going to college and working the swing shift at a nursing home, and the combination of the long hours and the nature of the work was badly depressing her. She felt she could no longer go on working there.

On the other hand I felt she had to keep the job. I did not

56

see how I could send her to college, plus take the financial responsibility for the additional car she needed for transportation.

Arriving at work very distraught, I asked the Lord to give me peace about the situation. As I prayed, I grew more bold in my prayers, finally crying out to the Lord, "I *must* have Your peace. I can't teach, feeling like this."

I continued praying, and shortly before school began the Lord spoke to my heart, "Her working there is not the only solution," He said.

That was all. Perhaps you are thinking that this was a rather self-evident thing for the Lord to say. Well, it was, but in my experience He frequently does say the obvious. It is the obvious that needs to be said and, much more importantly, the obvious that needs to be heard.

That one sentence was exactly what I needed to hear that morning. With it came the peace I wanted so badly. The burden was completely lifted—so completely lifted that a few days later I was able to tell Les to quit her job.

We all know of people who have the ability to say the right thing at the right time. How much more so is the Lord like that. A friend whose son was having enough trouble in school to jeopardize his graduation found herself getting terribly uptight about the situation. She felt trapped between two opposing forces. On the one side, she felt the school was pressuring her to do something about Tom and, on the other, the more she tried to discipline him the more he rebelled.

Each day she gave the problem to the Lord but each time a new complication arose she took it back. Then on two consecutive days the Lord gave her the Scripture, "All things work together for good to them that love God," (Rom. 8:28), first in a book she was reading, then through a guest speaker at her church.

She was as familiar with that verse as anyone. In fact, it was one of the first verses she had learned as a Christian, and she had frequently consoled herself with it. But when the Lord gave it to her that second time in church, it completely removed the weight she was carrying. It was suddenly gone and replaced with joy, and she was able to quit worrying about her son and his school problems. Even when Tom dropped out of school she did not lose that peace, and she is still trusting the Lord to help him grow up.

Psalm 112 speaks of the blessings of the man who delights in doing the Lord's commands, *"For he is settled in his mind that Jehovah will take care of him."*

If we are overcome by the circumstances we meet along the road, if we fear bad news or live in dread of what might happen, it is because we are *not* settled in our mind that Jesus will take care of us on this portion of our journey.

The whole Bible is a testimony of God's taking care of His children, and the fact that we don't really believe it proves, not His unfaithfulness but, rather, our unbelief.

Is there any secret to securing the Lord's blessing in our times of need? Yes, I believe there is and this is it: Stop resenting and blaming the Lord for the problems, the trials, the frustrations that come upon us. We live in a world where Satan and frequently our own disobedience play active roles. We have never been promised a life with no problems, but only that, in Jesus, we can have victory over those problems (cf. John 16:33).

When my friend Bonnie learned that her son was traveling with a crowd that was into alcohol and drugs, she did not bewail her situation or complain to the Lord, accusing the Lord of treating her unfairly. No, instead she went down on her knees, grateful that He was there to turn to in this hour of need, thanking Him for His love and comfort and the solution He would provide for the problem. She also asked Him to make her open to whatever He had to teach her through this situation.

Whenever I saw her during this time she was very much at peace and I believe it was her attitude of submission to the Lord that brought her son completely out of the drug scene within the next couple of months.

At all times, in every circumstance, we must have complete faith that, if we will let Him, the Lord can and will bring good out of these problems that provoke and frustrate us so much and cause us sorrow and discontent.

We, as single women, must learn to rely on the Lord completely.

What a glorious privilege that is—to test the promises of the Lord and learn firsthand that they are true, to learn again and again, until it is sure knowledge, that He indeed is faithful!

Remember, Lord, You promised,
"The seed of the righteous shall be delivered."

Chapter 5

WATCH OUT FOR CHILDREN

The book telling single women how to travel successfully through life with their children has not, to my knowledge, been written.

The books I have read in my search for counsel on single Christian parenthood were all written by men and intended for people who are a part of a complete family unit. They were written with the additional assumption that the reader would read the book while her children were very young. Unfortunately, they had little or nothing to say to mothers who are heads of their household and/or have half-grown children—children possibly badly scarred by divorce, death or separation.

So a large section of the Body of Christ must continue to wait until the Holy Spirit impresses upon someone to write the book these parents so desperately need.

I wish with all my heart that I had the knowledge to write such a book but I don't. In fact, the Lord has made it clear to me that I don't have even the knowledge to write a chapter on the subject.

When I first began this chapter I thought I could at least share my failures with you in the hope that you might learn from my mistakes. But as I was writing this well-intentioned piece of learning-through-hindsight, the Lord brought me to a place of such personal crisis in my family life that I knew I had far too little to offer any reader.

After the crisis, I believe that the Lord said to me, in effect, "My Word is sufficient." I believe He would have me share with you what He taught me and, which I originally shared in an article in Logos Digest, while I was going through a rough time with one of my daughters.

* * * * *

Is there a parent, Christian or non-Christian, alive today who is not concerned over her children? How are they going to turn out? Are they going to grow into the kind of adults we can relate to and respect? What does the future hold for them?

Certainly such anxiety is understandable. In an age when children are rejecting the standards, the morality, seemingly everything parents believe in, there is scarcely a home that is not touched by this spirit of rebellion. Even children brought up in the most sheltered Christian homes are frequently not immune to this disease of our age.

Yet I believe that God does not want us to be concerned over our children, if this concern causes anxiety, worry and tension. Jesus told us not to be "anxious about tomorrow," and this command concerns our children's tomorrows as well as our own. Even if these children choose to travel a different road by a heart-breaking set of rules, we can trust that somewhere up ahead, an all-loving Travel Guide has set up a detour that will lead them back to safety.

Recently when I felt I had good reason to be upset over one of my children, the Lord immediately gave me so much reassurance and peace in the form of Scripture (much of which I had never "seen" before or at least not seen in this light) about the position of children of Christians, that I was able to place the whole situation in His hands and whole-heartedly praise Him for its resolution, which was shortly forthcoming.

Since then I have been able to trust the Lord for the working out of my children's Salvation and sanctification, knowing that my prayers will be answered because they are prayed in the name of Jesus and the will of the Father.

I would like to share the Scripture the Lord gave me with the prayerful hope that it will be as revealing and comforting to you as it has been to me.

In reading the Old Testament, I have been struck by the fact that the Lord frequently worked through the house or household of His people. In Exodus 11:5,7, Moses reveals the Lord's plan and promise of Salvation for the Israelites. "And all the first-born in the land of Egypt shall die, from the first-born of Pharoah who sitteth upon his throne, even unto the first-born of the maidservant, who is behind the mill and all the beasts. But against any of the children of Israel shall not a dog move his tongue against man or beast; that ye may know that the Lord doth put a difference between the Egyptians and Israel."

In Exodus 12:3 the Lord commands Moses and Aaron, "Speak ye unto all the congregation of Israel saying, In the tenth day of this month they shall take to them every man a lamb, according to the house of their fathers, *a lamb for an house.*"

Exodus 12:12-13 continues, "For I will pass through the land of Egypt this night and will smite all the first-born in the land of Egypt, both man and beast; and against all the gods of Egypt I will execute judgment: I am the Lord.

"And the blood shall be to you for a token upon the houses where ye are; and when I see the blood, I will pass over you, and the plague shall not be upon you to destroy you, when I smite the land of Egypt."

Exodus 12:23: "For the Lord will pass through to smite

the Egyptians; and when he seeth the blood upon the lintel and on the two side posts, the Lord will pass over the door and *will not suffer the destroyer to come into your houses to smite you.*"

Now, the lamb of the Passover is, of course, Jesus Christ and today, Christians are the spiritual Israelites and can claim all the promises given to the original Israelites. While I do not suggest in any way that belief in Jesus on the part of parents can actually provide Salvation for their children, I do believe these passages indicate that the children of the household are somehow protected and kept safe by the blood of Jesus until Jesus can reveal Himself to them.

There is a plague in Egypt (the world) today, but I believe that God will not permit the destroyer to come into the house of Christians to smite them if they will only have confidence in Him for this protection. Truly, the Lord does make a distinction between the children of Israel (Christians) and the Egyptians (non-believers).

This same idea is conveyed in I Corinthians 7:14 when Paul writes that the unbelieving husband or wife is set apart by the believing partner. "Otherwise your children would be unclean [unblessed heathen, outside the Christian covenant] but as it is, they are prepared for God—pure and clean." (Amp.)

In Joshua 2:18 we again see an entire family protected and kept safe by the faith and actions of one of its members—Rahab. "Behold when we come into the land, thou shalt bind this line of scarlet thread [Jesus' blood] in the window by which thou didst let us down; and thou shalt bring thy father and thy mother and thy brethren and all thy father's household, home unto thee."

That the parent can speak for the household is evident by Joshua's statement in Joshua 24:15, "But as for me, and my house, we will serve the Lord."

The Old Testament abounds in promises for parents concerning their children. Here are a few of my favorites:

Proverbs 11:21: "But the seed of the righteous shall be delivered." The righteous—that's you and me. We are the righteous, those who have right standing with God, through Christ, and our seed is our children.

"And it shall come to pass afterward, that I will pour out my Spirit upon all flesh; *and your sons and your daughters shall prophesy . . ."* (Joel 2:28)

"Wherefore it shall come to pass, if ye hearken to these judgments and keep, and do them, that the Lord thy God shall keep unto thee the covenant and the mercy which he swore unto thy fathers. And He will love thee and bless thee and multiply thee; *he will also bless the fruit of thy womb . . ."* (Deut. 7:12-13)

Children in the Bible are frequently referred to as fruit, and I especially like the promise in Malachi 3:10. "Bring all the tithes into the storehouse that there may be food in mine house, and prove me now herewith, saith the Lord of hosts, if I will not open for you the windows of heaven and pour out for you a blessing, that there shall not be room enough to receive it. *And I will rebuke the devourer for your sakes and he shall not destroy the fruits of your ground."*

As a tither I believe I can claim this verse for my children. What can happen to them with God Himself there to rebuke Satan?

Similar promises in the New Testament are a little harder to find but they are there. The Lord showed me two in particular, which have become some of my favorite passages in all Scripture.

"The leader of the local synagogue, whose name was Jairus, came and fell down before him, pleading with him to heal his little daughter. 'She is at the point of death,' he said in desperation. 'Please come and place your hands on her and make her live.' And Jesus went with him . . .

"While he was still talking . . . messengers arrived from Jairus' home with the news that it was too late—his daughter was dead and there was no point in Jesus' coming now. But Jesus ignored their comments and said to Jairus,

'Don't be afraid. Just trust me.' Then Jesus halted the crowd and wouldn't let anyone go on with him to Jairus' home except Peter and James and John. When they arrived, Jesus saw that all was in great confusion, with unrestrained weeping and wailing. He went inside and spoke to the people.

" 'Why all this weeping and commotion?' he asked. 'The child isn't dead; she is only asleep!' They laughed at him in bitter derision, but he told them all to leave, and taking the little girl's father and mother and his three disciples, he went into the room where she was lying.

"Taking her by the hand he said to her, 'Get up, little girl!' (She was twelve years old.) And she jumped up and walked around! Her parents just couldn't get over it. Jesus instructed them very earnestly not to tell what had happened, and told them to give her something to eat." (Mark 5:22-24, 35-43 TLB)

This is what these passages say to me. Sometimes we see our children as spiritually dead. We plead with Jesus, and because He has compassion for us, He tries to tell us they are only asleep. "Don't be afraid. Just trust me." We, of course, don't hear or believe Him. Then when we and all our friends and neighbors are completely convinced there is no hope, Jesus touches these "dead" children and, at His touch, they awaken (come alive spiritually). His only command to us at the time of their awakening is to give them (spiritual) food.

The second story is from John.

"In the course of his journey through Galilee he arrived at the town of Cana, where he had turned the water into wine. While he was there, a man in the city of Capernaum, a government official, whose son was very sick, heard that Jesus had come from Judea and was traveling in Galilee. This man went over to Cana, found Jesus, and begged him to come to Capernaum with him and heal his son, who was now at death's door.

"Jesus asked, 'Won't any of you believe in me unless I do more and more miracles?'

"The official pled, 'Sir, please come now before my child dies.'

"Then Jesus told him, 'Go back home. Your son is healed!' And the man believed Jesus and started home.

> While he was on his way, some of his servants met him with the news that all was well—his son had recovered. He asked them when the lad had begun to feel better, and they replied, 'Yesterday afternoon at about one o'clock his fever suddenly disappeared!' Then the father realized it was the same moment that Jesus had told him, 'Your son is healed.' And the officer and his entire household believed that Jesus was the Messiah." (John 4:46-53 TLB)

When we come to Jesus with our complaints and fears about our children who are spiritually at death's door, He sometimes reproves us, saying, "Unless you see miracles, (unless your children are dancing in the Spirit, speaking in tongues and prophesying) you won't believe."

Jesus, who can look into the hearts of our children and see into the future says, "Your son is healed."

Can we, like the nobleman, believe the word Jesus has spoken?

The promises the Lord has given us are as much for today as they were for the day they were written.

What must we do to see them fulfilled in our children's lives? I believe there are seven steps to take.

1. We must believe that it is God's will that our children be saved.

2. We must give our children to the Lord and then believe that He will move sovereignly in their lives because we have entrusted them to Him.

3. We must ask the Lord for their Salvation in Jesus' Name and, as the priest of the household, claim their protection meanwhile.

4. We must leave the way and the time the Lord brings them to Salvation up to Him and stop telling Him how and when it should be done.

5. We must believe God has initiated the process by which our prayer is being answered no matter what the external circumstances say.

6. We must continually thank the Lord and praise Him for that Salvation.

7. We should remind the Lord of His promises whenever we find ourselves doubting and continue to praise Him for their fulfillment.

Our Travel Agent has never promised that there will be no storms, but we can count on His help as we journey through the turbulence of raising children.

Well, Lord, what do You want me to do now?

70

Chapter 6

ROAD
BLOCK

Amy and Bill were married while he was still in college. A highly-skilled secretary, Amy worked while Bill attended medical school and she continued working until he had set up a practice. Only then did she stay home to have their family—three children in four years.

Very busy with the young children, Amy did not realize at first just how much time Bill was spending away from home. She credited his busyness to his growing practice.

When Bill confronted her with a demand for a divorce Amy was taken by surprise, stunned by his accusations that he needed a wife who could "challenge him mentally and discuss something more interesting than diapers, toilet training and preschool."

She stood by helplessly through the divorce proceedings, too numb to put up a fight. When she could feel again, her dominant emotions were bitterness against her former husband and his "mentally-challenging" second wife, and anger, directed against God "who would let something like this happen to me."

Janet and Bud grew up together in the church. Sweethearts from their early teen years, they were married immediately after graduation from high school. On their honeymoon, Bud was killed in a boating accident.

Today, Janet spends much time reliving her life before Bud's death. "Don't tell me about God," she lashes out angrily to anyone who tries to comfort her. "I'll never trust Him again. He's supposed to be all-powerful; if He had wanted to, He could have stopped Bud from getting killed."

Rose comes from a large outgoing family. Although she dated a lot when she was younger and even had two "serious" romances, neither led to marriage. Today she lives with her aging father and has almost no social life. She especially avoids family functions because her jealousy of her married brothers and sisters keeps her from enjoying herself and makes her poor company.

Although Rose seldom discusses her feelings with anyone else she, too, secretly holds God responsible for her unhappy state. "God could have sent me a husband instead of condemning me to this kind of life," she once confided to a friend. "If God really cared about me, He'd care about my happiness, too."

Who do you blame for the problems and heartache in your life?

When you're forced to make an unexpected detour or even travel over a road that looks remarkably like one you've been on before, do you question God's love and sovereignty? Because you've accepted Jesus do you believe He's responsible for everything that happens to you—good, bad and indifferent? What about the boyfriend or husband who did you wrong, your rebellious children who show you no gratitude, the friend who betrayed you? Did they all act according to some secret, little-understood plan of God?

Who is the scapegoat in your life?

Some Christians are living testimonies of the fact that they hold God accountable for the misery and unpleasantness in their lives. Many of us seem to have trouble recognizing the real villain of the universe.

The cardinal rule in any kind of warfare is to know who the enemy is, so let's make one thing clear right now. If you have problems in your life, there are *three* possible reasons. Let's take a look at each of them.

When a woman becomes a Christian, she should accept Jesus in two distinct roles:

1. that of Savior, the Son of God, whose death on the cross has paid the full price for all her sins and made her acceptable to the Father, and

2. that of Lord who, as her Master, has exclusive rights to all her time, energy and service.

Most of us don't have too much trouble with the Savior role of Jesus but our acceptance of it just gets us started on our Christian walk. It doesn't equip us for the long days and nights of travel ahead. However, when it comes to accepting Jesus as our Lord and Master, well, that's a different story.

Jesus has made it very plain that we can't serve two masters (cf. Matt. 6:24). If we aren't serving Jesus, there's only one power left to serve—Satan—the ruler of the darkness of the world. Yes, I said Satan, that old master of deception. His two greatest deceptions have been first, to convince people that he doesn't exist and second, that there's a gray area, a kind of spiritual no-man's land, where neither God nor Satan reign.

If you are *not* serving God and, therefore, *are* serving Satan, you are very much at his mercy and it is no wonder that you have problems. A trouble-filled life is your heritage from him. Even if you are unwittingly serving him, for example, in one of the cults, the occult or other satanic activities you are still at his mercy. God has expressly said that such practices are offensive to Him (cf. Deut. 18:10-12).

So widespread are Satan's activities in this world that the most devout Christian is not immune from their influence.

Death, sickness—catastrophes of all kinds—are the work of the power of darkness.

Am I really saying that Satan can bother a Christian?

Yes, I am.

But isn't God supposed to be all-powerful?

Yes, He is, but He has deliberately limited His power here on earth.

Does that mean the Christian is completely vulnerable to Satan's activities?

No, it doesn't. When Jesus returned to heaven, He gave His power to His followers to use in spiritual warfare (cf. Matt. 28:18-20, Mark 16:15-18), and any time a Christian feels her problems are due to Satan she can bind him and cast him out of the situation in the Name of Jesus. If she repents, stands firm, and doesn't give Satan any further foothold in her life, that will take care of him.

The second enemy that plagues a Christian is "self." I may well be a new creation, but there is a lot of the old me hanging around yet.

The Christian walk is a matter of continually giving more and more of ourselves to the Lord and those uncommitted areas of our lives can give us a lot of trouble. God has given us free will and, as Christian women, we can deliberately sin. We can and often do make poor choices in our daily living if we haven't appropriated the wisdom the Lord is ready to give us (cf. Jam. 1:5).

Take, for example, a woman like Joan who, though she knew better, married Dan, a non-Christian with the hope of converting him later. Dan, however, has shown no interest in becoming a Christian. He prefers his way of living and is frequently angry with Joan because she won't share its "joys." No matter how much Joan would blame God for not making her marriage work, it was her own willful act that created the situation in the first place.

There are also many people like Linda, who "fudge just a little" on their income taxes. Three years ago, Linda was audited by the Internal Revenue and asked to explain some of the items on her tax forms. The questioning resulted in Linda's paying a fine, plus some back taxes. Now her tax forms are audited each year by the IRS. Can she blame Satan for her "harassment"? Of course not. In this instance, Linda listened to "self," rather than following God's invitation to a higher level of conduct.

The third possible reason for some of the trouble we experience is frequently a cause of confusion to many people. We have difficulty understanding that, as the Holy Spirit works to bring order out of the chaos in lives, He sometimes will temporarily allow unpleasant, sorrowful, even potentially shattering experiences to happen to us.

In order to understand this we must understand the nature of the love God bears us. Since our Lord's ultimate purpose is "to do [us] good in the end," (Deut. 8:16 Amp.) His love cannot permit us to live life at nursery school level.

Does that sound strange?

I'll try to explain.

Human love is perhaps best described as sentimentality. Human parents are moved by their children's tears, complaints, sulking, depression, so that they frequently give in to them and allow the children to do things that aren't good for them.

God's love isn't like that. When a Christian woman puts God in charge and makes Jesus Lord of her life, then she can trust God to do whatever is best for her, no matter how much she cries, fusses, complains or sulks, no matter how much it hurts.

You see, God has one main purpose for Christian women—to make us mature daughters.

He achieves His purpose in a variety of ways. Before we are Christians He lets us choose our own route because that's probably the quickest way to getting us in a position where we make such a mess of our lives that if we have any sense at all, we'll turn to Him for help.

Once we accept Him as Savior He has a different job. If we still haven't accepted Him as Lord, He has to show us that that is the next step.

Most of us know Christians who complain, "I can't get away with anything." A young friend was driving home after midnight. She was on a completely deserted residential street so she decided that no one would be the wiser if she exceeded the speed limit. She had no sooner accelerated the engine than a police car pulled out of "nowhere" and her little act of disobedience cost her the price of one speeding ticket.

We've all heard this kind of story or had it happen to us too often to believe that it's coincidence. I believe it's just God's way of letting us know who's in charge, even when we think we're getting away with something.

Sometimes, Christians will discover that their lives are a lot rougher since they became believers. "I never had so many problems as a non-Christian," a friend at church complained.

This may very well be the truth for a new Christian or even at times for any Christian. If this is your story, think of yourself as the dwelling place of the Holy Spirit. Right now He may be engaging in some very much needed housecleaning. Everyone knows how dreadful a place looks in the middle of a cleaning job. But, afterwards, the results are worth the temporary disruption and disorder.

Once God gets us where He wants us—recognizing and accepting Jesus as Lord—He still has a job to do in us, a big job if He is to perfect us. He accomplishes this perfecting through several methods. His ways may seem the same to the non-discerning eye, but I think it is important that the Christian understand how the Lord is working in her life.

The Lord is exquisitely creative and His methods of perfecting us as we trek along together are infinite but, for now, let's consider two very important ones: chastening and pruning.

The writer of Hebrews reminds us, "For whom the Lord loveth, he chasteneth and scourgeth every son whom he receiveth. If ye endure chastening God dealeth with you as with sons; . . . but he [chasteneth us] for our profit that we might be partakers of his holiness. Now no chastening for the present seemeth to be joyous, but grievous, nevertheless, afterward it yieldeth the peaceable fruit of righteousness unto them who are exercised by it." (Heb. 12:6-7, 10-11)

Our Heavenly Father chastens us when we've been disobedient in much the same way an earthly father would if an earthly father were all-wise, all-loving and all-powerful. You see, God knows this "game" of life is played for very high stakes.

Of course, chastening can be part of the sowing and reaping process with the nature of the punishment built into the act, itself. The Bible warns us about being gluttonous and, if we eat too much, we get fat and open our bodies to any number of accompanying diseases.

God tells us not to be drunkards and, if we drink too much, we may bring ruination to our bodies and possibly our minds as well. We are warned about letting the sun go down on our wrath, the love of money, fornication and that, if we are disobedient, we must pay the price in one way or another. Most sin carries its own form of built-in punishment.

Don't be fooled by the lies of the world. God is in the business of building His eternal family and He will not let anything stand in His way, especially not us. He will do whatever is needed to mold us closer to the image of Jesus—allow a marriage to be turned upside down, end a job, permit friends to become enemies, reveal us for what we really are, let us suffer the consequences of our own actions—all just to bring us closer to the point where we will turn around to Him and say, "Forgive me, Father. I'll do it Your way next time."

Let me give you a very simple analogy. Think of a very loving parent, a surgeon, who discovers in his own child a terrible cancer. The cancer must be cut out. Now the surgeon truly loves his child and he knows the surgery is painful. But he also knows the child will die without it. Certainly, he will subject his child to that operation no matter how much the child may beg him not to.

Our Father knows that unrepented sin is like a cancer and allowing it to grow can eventually result in our spiritual death, so He subjects us to His surgery, even when it is necessarily painful.

Another way the Lord accomplishes His perfection is by pruning us. Jesus said, "Every branch in me that beareth not fruit he taketh away; and every branch that beareth fruit, he purgeth it, that it may bring forth more fruit." (John 15:2) All of us have felt the pruning shears of our Heavenly Father. Fortunately we have, in our Father, a master gardener who knows what He is doing. Jesus tells us that the Father removes two kinds of branches, those that bear no fruit and those that do, for even greater bearing.

I have a row of rose bushes in my backyard. Unfortunately, the soil in which they are planted is very poor. The roses are relatively unprotected where they are growing and, as I am no gardener, they are also neglected. Every year the branches become more spindly, the entire plant a little weaker and sicker. However, if you were to judge by the flowers they produce, you would never guess they came from sick plants. But no matter how beautiful the flowers are, one fact is inescapable. The plants on which they grow are dying.

The only thing that could save those roses is an "operation" at the hands of a master gardener. Yet, I can imagine if the plants themselves were consulted about the possibility of being pruned back they might protest, "But look at the beautiful flowers we're producing."

How many of us are like those rose plants when the Father comes to prune us? We are so busy admiring our outward appearances that we have blinded ourselves to spiritual, death-producing diseases in our bodies and souls.

We serve a God who lets nothing go to waste; this is especially true during the so-called problem times of our lives.

Romans 8:28 emphasizes the Lord's ability to bring good out of every situation for those "that love God, to them who are called according to his purpose."

James counsels us, "Is your life full of difficulties and temptations? Then be happy, for when the way is rough, your patience has a chance to grow. So let it grow, and don't try to squirm out of your problems. For when your patience is finally in full bloom, then you will be ready for anything, strong in character, full and complete." (Jam. 1:2 TLB)

Peter admonishes: "These trials are only to test your faith, to see whether or not it is strong and pure. It is being tested as fire tests gold and purifies it—and your faith is far more precious to God than mere gold; so if your faith remains strong after being tried in the test tube of fiery trials, it will bring you much praise and glory and honor on the day of his return." (I Pet. 1:7 TLB)

Of course, it's difficult, even painful, when we find ourselves in situations where people mistreat us or circumstances seem beyond our ability to bear, but it is through situations such as these that the Lord observes our reliance on Him and can see what is in our hearts (cf. II Chron. 32:31). At the worst of times we can be encouraged because, "There hath no temptation taken you, but such as is common to man; but God is faithful, who will not suffer you to be tempted above that ye are able, but will with the temptation also make a way to escape that ye may be able to bear it." (I Cor. 10:13)

I believe it is important for the Christian woman to discern what God is doing in her life at any particular time in order that she may make the best possible response.

If the Lord is chastening us, what do we do? Well, we should respond in exactly the way we feel our children should respond to our punishment—by admitting our guilt and repenting of it. Our reaction to punishment may also condition its severity. If we quickly see our mistake and tell God we're sorry, that may be the end of it right then. But if we fight back and revile God we'll only hurt ourselves.

If we discern that, instead of punishing us, God is doing some pruning in our lives we shouldn't hinder His cutting process. Most likely, He is either removing dead wood (and who needs it?), pruning for our health's sake or pruning for a greater yield of spiritual fruit in our lives. We should never resist God's cutting, but praise Him for it, even if it hurts.

Should we discern that we are being tested, we should use all the resources at hand to pass that test. Trusting that He is a loving Father, praising Him and giving Him our full cooperation should earn us a passing grade.

Finally, if we will stop blaming our troubles on God and recognize our own and Satan's responsibility in the "bad deals" in our lives, we are entitled to the "fringe benefit" that the Lord gives with this knowledge.

When we look beyond the people and situations that seemingly cause our problems then we can recognize them for what they are or can be—instruments in the working out of our perfection. And that just could include the girl who walked off with the neatest guy you ever met, your parent who doesn't understand your need for privacy, or the boss who doesn't properly appreciate you.

You don't have to take what they do or don't do to you personally any longer. You don't have to hate, be bitter, feel angry, resentful, humiliated or defeated. In fact, you no longer need harbor any negative emotions toward anybody ever again.

You don't have to look around for anyone to blame at all.

And that is worth the price of your learner's permit.

I'm so yielded to the Lord I bet He can hardly believe it!

Chapter 7

YIELD

RIGHT

OF

WAY

I was good and mad at the Lord and His whole Travel Agency!

As I got ready for work that morning I mentally ticked off the reasons.

No. 1: Pressure! No. 2: Pressure! No. 3: Pressure!

How much did the Lord think I could take? At school my yearbook staff was considerably behind its deadline. At the same time the newspaper class was in the throes of putting out its next issue.

At home, my male cat had a bladder infection and was attempting to "water down" the whole house, especially my relatively-new orange rug. The night before the dishwasher had made an unattractive sound and then gone on strike.

The absence of anything appetizing with which to make my lunch reminded me that I needed to go food shopping and that in turn triggered off the ever-haunting knowledge that, for the moment, my family's expenditures were more than my income, and the small inheritance left by my mother, which gave me so much mental pleasure every time I contemplated my bankbook, was dwindling fast away.

There, too, in the dark recesses of my consciousness was the ever-present question of my daughters' relationship with the Lord.

As I put on my coat, the sight of Leslie's pick-up out the window reminded me that the truck was a very reluctant starter in the cold spell we were having. The day before, by the time Les had gotten it started, she had managed to miss her first class at college, a class that car trouble and inclement weather had caused her to miss all too frequently.

Complicating the picture was my headache, a headache that started below my shoulders and was so encompassing it seemed to continue on out to my hair ends.

As I mentally reviewed my day's schedule the crux of my anger revealed itself. The real reason I was mad at the Lord was our continuing battle over time. And here I felt my anger was justified. Just what did the Lord think I was made of? For the past twelve years I had been so busy it seemed like I never really had any time to call my own. I had been busy working, busy going to school, busy raising children, busy keeping house, busy doing them altogether, and I was tired of it. I was tired of having so little time for myself, time just to sit down and watch a TV program, go to a movie, read something light, coffee klatch with friends or just sit around doing nothing without feeling guilty, tired of not ever having a few minutes a day I could call my own. (It really isn't fair, Lord, and what's more You know it isn't fair.)

My burdens, anger, pain and I all headed for the door. But the morning held one last surprise for me. Just in front of the door I almost stepped into two of the largest masses of dog vomit I had ever seen in my life.

At this point, you are probably wondering why I am "blessing" you with all these gory details. No, my purpose is not to show you that lovely, sweet-smelling, Spirit-filled "I" have problems, too. I have another more important purpose.

I'm sure that most of us have reached a point in the road similar to the one I've described. And, when we do, there are any number of ways we can react to such a multiple crises situation the Lord has let us wander into:

We can become angry and probably make the situation worse, plus take on the added burden of bitterness;

We can become depressed and, while the situation may or may not become any worse, it will certainly loom larger in our minds;

We can give up and herin lies the way to despair and mental illness;

OR

We can admit that somehow we haven't followed our Guide closely enough and *we can give in!*

That's what I did that morning.

I suddenly saw the humor of the whole situation. I do not pretend to have any special wisdom into the workings of God's mind, but through experience I do know that one way the Lord works in my life is by what I call the pressure-cooker method. By this, I mean, that when the Lord is trying to teach me something that I am unwilling or reluctant to learn, He piles more and more pressure on, and He continues to pour it on until I either learn the lesson or am at least ready to begin learning it.

So that cold, dark, unpromising morning, I finally became miserable enough to respond to the Lord.

I could laugh because I really was in a pretty silly situation. Have you ever seen a small child, about two years old, stand up to his father? Daddy is displeased about something the child has done and gives him a whack. The child gives Daddy a look and hits back. This can go on until Daddy either gives the child a whack that shows he really means business, or else he lets the kid win the round. I have always marveled at the incredible nerve of a small child hitting a father who could physically demolish him if he were so inclined.

I have seen some fathers who were amused when this

happened in their families. They admired the kid's "spunk" and made sure they didn't break that spirit.

Fortunately, God is not that kind of father. He is neither amused nor intrigued by any kind of rebelliousness in His children. Be assured, if we respond to God's dealing with any form of rebellion, He will not walk away with an amused smile on His face, secretly chuckling to Himself over His "high-spirited" child. If we have refused to learn the lesson the Lord feels we are ready to learn when He feels we are ready to learn it, He'll be back sooner or later (probably sooner) with installment number two.

But back to my morning crisis. As you may have already concluded, I had some other things to do besides clean up the mess. The Lord was obviously spotlighting a very important area in my life, and saying in essence, "Jo Anne, get with it."

As I said before, I gave in—I mentally made a U-turn and resurrendered myself and every part of my life to Him—including my pretty new rug that I had so hoped would stay clean. If that rug had to be stained, soiled, even ruined to teach me to stop putting so much attention on material things, then so be it.

I gave up the idea of a dishwasher that worked. I resurrendered my children, their future, their Salvation, everything about them to the Lord. They were His problem. If He wanted my daughter to go to college on a certain day He'd get her there. If He wanted her in college at all, He'd take care of that, too.

Regarding the girls' relationship with Him, I vowed to stand on His Word. He has promised the "seed of the righteous" shall be delivered. I am righteous by virtue of the blood of Jesus. I decided to stop fretting and have faith in God's ability to draw my children into His perfect will for them.

Next, I told the Lord my finances were up to Him. He is my source and my substance. I put the yearbook and the newspaper deadlines in His hands. Whether we made the deadlines or not was entirely up to Him.

That brought us to the heart of my rebellion—the matter of time. With a real effort I finally surrendered that to Him, too, and all my "rights" concerning it. Goodbye, television; goodbye, movies; goodbye, trivial reading; goodbye, casual friendships; goodbye, everything that the Lord decides I don't need in my life.

The following days were literally as different from the crisis period just past as night is from day. Just as the past week had been one of frustration, the next was filled with peace. It seemed almost as though I had only to hold out my hand and the Lord filled it.

My department chairman told me of a change of program for the next semester that would cut my work load considerably. I opened a book I hadn't looked at for months and found the "perfect" assignment for my next day's English class.

A student who had been rude came and apologized.

A photographer dropped off some pictures, saving me a time-consuming trip.

A rebellious class settled down and actually worked quietly.

Needless to say my headache departed.

My animals recovered from their assorted illnesses. Deadlines were met. I said a half-hearted prayer over the dishwasher, cleaned it out, tinkered around with it, and it began to run as well as ever.

Through a good mechanic we found out what was wrong with my daughter's car and we had it fixed.

What was the Lord teaching me through all of this? A whole package of things actually. But the really big lesson He had been trying to teach me was that when I accepted Him as Lord of my life, that included His being Lord over everything and especially over my time.

You see, we Christians have been purchased by Jesus, and that doesn't make us "servants" as the King James' writers interpreted the word in Galatians 1:10, but rather "slaves." The idea of slavery isn't very popular with modern women. We like to believe we are independent and free. But in this idea we are deceived. Life has never been a question of slavery versus freedom. It has only been a question of slavery versus slavery, and the only choice anyone gets to make is whose slave she's going to be—Jesus' or Satan's.

There's no room for "me" in either camp, no time in my life when I belong to myself. Anyone who mistakenly thinks she's doing her own thing is really doing Satan's thing.

When Jesus freed me from Satan's possession He bought me completely—all my time included. The Lord knows that any time I supposedly spend for me is not only wasted time, but in my particular case, time when I can get into trouble.

Does this mean I never watch TV, go to movies, etc? Well, that's a funny thing. Once I surrendered my time to the Lord, there suddenly was extra time, time when I could watch TV if I wanted to. And that brings us to another amazing thing. I no longer really cared whether I watched it or not.

Please understand. We are all individuals. The Lord may never ask you to give up television or movies or anything like that. He works through different means in each of our lives. And remember, that the real battle in my life was over time. Once I made Jesus Lord in that area, He returned some of it to me.

Let me add one more point. I am convinced that when it is necessary, the Lord will do anything, permit us to go through anything and apply incredible pressure to our lives, just to bring us to the position where He can deal with us.

Then when He can deal with us, when we are ready to acknowledge Him as Lord in all areas (even time) we learn, usually to our surprise, that this life of slavery, which we had been falsely deceived into thinking would be painful and restrictive, is actually the life of freedom. Only this freedom is not the world's concept of freedom—doing our own thing—but the freedom that comes from doing His will.

Okay, Lord, I'll dump the whole works!

Chapter 8

Invariably, when a group of single women feels really comfortable together, one question comes up: What about sex?

Far more often, however, the question remains unspoken, for, as supposedly "liberated" as American women are in the area of sex, many Christians are as bound as their Victorian forefathers.

It is no exaggeration, I believe, to say that no subject is thought about more and discussed less by Christian single women than sex.

I hope the knowledge that you are not the only single woman in the Kingdom who experiences keen sexual desire will be a liberating one for you.

No, you are not some kind of sexual pervert if:

more often than you would ever admit you lie awake at night wondering what sex is like or poignantly remembering what it was like;

if you are embarrassed, shocked, repulsed by some sexual

thoughts that come unbidden to your mind;

if the sight of an attractive man occasionally (or not so occasionally) sets your glands to working;

if you masturbate (no matter how guilty it makes you feel).

Only in the very last few years has the Church seen fit to recognize that our sexuality is God-given. But although there have been some excellent Christian books on sex published recently, they are largely aimed at sexuality within the framework of marriage, and the unmarried woman is usually counseled with the simple admonition, "Don't." Should the single state and sex be considered at all, there is little attempt made to tell her "how *not* to."

Such lack of consideration has led to much frustration on the part of a large number of single women who, if they find themselves unable to cope with their own sexual desires, are somehow left with the impression that there must be something wrong with them because they're obviously the only people in the whole world who have not made an adequate adjustment.

As one friend put it, "Being single and having sexual desire must be a lot like having a third arm. It must be good for something, but what?"

Since the subject of sex, particularly among single women, is still largely taboo in many churches, the single woman with concerns or serious problems is often left with few resources. For almost any other problem there is some kind of help or counseling available but, if her problem is sexual in nature, where can she go?

Consulting a non-Christian psychologist can be even more dangerous than useless. There is no other area in which the world and the Church are further apart than they are in the area of sexual standards. And the misguided woman who is foolish enough to consult a non-Christian psychologist may be led to "understand" that her real problem is her "narrow religious beliefs," as a Christian acquaintance of mine was told.

On the other hand, Christian psychologists who might have a lot to contribute in this area are hard to find.

What about her own minister? The answer is probably "no" again. Most ministers are not adequately trained, and frequently reluctant as well, to counsel women on sexual matters. Being male, and most likely married, they may not have much insight into her problem. Besides, it is questionable whether any man or woman not married to each other should discuss sexual matters to any degree.

It would seem that the best answer to the problem of available and adequate counseling for the single woman on the matter of sex is mature single women in the local church who are knowledgeable in related Scripture and have learned how to successfully deal with their own sexuality.

But if this kind of counseling is available, it is not generally known. So, the single woman of today must do what her sisters of other ages have always done; rely on what God has said on the matter and lean on the power of the Holy Spirit to walk this single road in accordance with God's Word.

But there is no cause for despair. This is probably still the best possible approach to take.

That being the case, let's look at what God has said on the subject.

In I Thessalonians 4:3, Paul tells us, "For this is the will of God, even your sanctification, that ye should abstain from fornication."

"Know ye not that the unrighteous shall not inherit the kingdom of God. Be not deceived, neither fornicators . . . shall inherit the kingdom of God." (I Cor. 6:9-10)

Fornication is defined as voluntary sexual intercourse on the part of an unmarried person with a person of the opposite sex. The Bible makes it absolutely clear that God is completely unbending on this subject. All sexual relations between men and women not married to each other are taboo, so taboo, in fact, that the Old Testament solution to the violation was usually stoning. That ought to give us a fair idea of how strongly God feels about the subject.

Yet, despite this very clearly defined instruction, we see many violations today, not only on the part of the younger generation with their man-made standards, but also in more mature people who ought to know better. And their excuse, with minor variations, is usually something like: "God understands and forgives us"; or, "Love makes it all right"; or again that oldie, "In the eyes of God we're married."

If you are being or ever have been deceived by these lies of Satan, flee to your nearest Bible and read first-hand what God has to say about fornication, and believe that He wouldn't say it if He didn't mean it.

While you're at it, don't start looking for Scripture that you can twist to suit your own purposes. You might come up with something like an acquaintance did, when she wanted to justify her moving in with her boyfriend. A Christian, she explained it this way: "God is love and since sex is one aspect of love, sex is of God. We're in love, so our having a sexual life together is of God."

About this time, I can "hear" many single women silently screaming, "But why is God so unfair? Why is He so dead set against an unmarried person having a sexual relationship?"

I think I can explain at least one very important reason.

What two categories of things are surrounded by the most safe-guards, have the most rules concerning their use? I think that you'll agree that they are the *dangerous* and the *precious*. Sex is certainly both of these.

Sex is one of the most explosive forces in the world. Wars have been fought, the history of nations changed, fortunes lost and lives ruined all because of sex.

Sex is also one of the most valuable forces. Through the sexual act life, itself, is conceived and through this union a man and a woman truly become one (cf. Gen. 2:24).

God is saying, in effect, that sex is too dangerous and too precious to be played with, to be careless with. So He has laid down very stringent rules for its use. The only safe place the sexual act can be performed is within the bonds of marriage.

Oh, I know the "prophets of the world" tell us we are "mature" enough to handle sex on our own. They are even telling us women that we can raise children well without a husband's help.

But that isn't what God says. And because He knows so well how difficult it is for a single person, particularly a single woman, to handle sexual relations, He has made His position very clear in the Bible.

Now that we've taken a look at God's "immovable" stand on sex, let's look at His "impossible" demands.

The Bible points out that refraining from the actual sexual act is only a small part of the story. God also warns against lasciviousness, inciting lust, (Mark 7:22); sensuality, excessive indulgence in sensual pleasures, (Jude 19); evil concupiscence, illicit desire, (Col. 3:5); defrauding (I Thes. 4:6); reprobation and being morally depraved (Rom. 1:28).

The Bible uses some very big words to express God's admonition that all forms of sexual practice, physical or mental, are out of bounds for the unmarried.

In the Old Testament God's people were forbidden to commit fornication. Then along came Jesus, who said we're just as guilty if we willfully *think* about committing it.

And that means no sex, period. No romantic daydreaming about real or imagined lotharios ready to sweep us off our feet and carry us away from this "wretched life of singleness"; no secret attachment for our doctor, lawyer, minister or our neighbor's husband; no harmless flirtations with the guy at the office (even though you both know it's a game).

You see, what Jesus knew and was telling us is that lust usually begins in the mind and if we can keep the idea out of our minds we'll have a lot less trouble with our bodies.

Now we can fuss and fume, feel cheated and experience a whole host of rebellious emotions. However, it is my firm conviction that the sooner we accept God's will on the matter, the sooner we can settle down to making a success of our lives at being the women He created us to be.

This may seem like a terribly hard-nosed stand on the subject but I believe it is the only stand that will allow you to be successfully single. I've tried many other routes—the daydreaming bit, the secret admiration from afar, the meaningless flirtations—and they all led down the same path, a preoccupation with sex that consumed an awful lot of time and energy and made me very dissatisfied with my lot in life.

All of this brings us to another question single women are concerned with. If all "outside" encounters with sex are "verboten," what about masturbation? After all, it only concerns yourself. Is it wrong, too? Isn't it better to masturbate occasionally than to spend a sleepless night or feel all keyed up?

I recently picked up a book in a Bible store to read what a Christian leader I admire had to say on this subject. He expressed the opinion that masturbation was a God-given means of release that could be used to carry people through some difficult times when they might otherwise commit fornication or adultery.

I can't argue with this writer. In general, Scripture does not have very much to say about masturbation, but I strongly believe that anyone who practices masturbation is definitely settling for God's second best in her life.

To my knowledge, masturbation is not usually a purely physical act; it is often accompanied by lustful thoughts, and even if masturbation is not expressly forbidden by the Bible, the lustful thoughts are. Why allow lust any entrance into our souls when we are striving for victory there?

So it looks very much like we're right back where we started. If fornication and all its accompanying stepsisters are denied the single Christian women, what does she do, where does she go, should lust or desire torment her?

Where would she go except to Jesus? Just as His death made provision for all the problems in our life, so I believe it made provision for illicit sexual desires as well.

If you will permit Him, Jesus can remove all sexual desire from your mind or body, as He did for a friend of mine who was married for over 20 years before she separated from her husband. When she gave her problem to Jesus, He completely removed all her sexual desire. Or He will, as He has for other women, give you control over your desires. Several women have told me that, although they still experience sexual desire, sometimes quite keenly, the Lord keeps it from becoming a problem to them.

Yes, His grace is sufficient whether it is given once and for all or on a daily basis (cf. II Cor. 12:9). The amount of grace given depends only upon our attitude. If we are willing to surrender forever, if need be, all our rights to sex in any of its mental or physical forms, then the Lord will give us grace for that. However, if we feel cheated because we are denied sex, or if we want to play games with sex and hold back the commitment of this area from God, then we probably won't get too much grace from Him in return.

In my own life, when I surrendered sex completely to the Lord, it was absolutely no problem, but when I "fudged" even a little on something as seemingly harmless as romantic daydreaming, I quickly found myself spending more and more time thinking about sex and just generally being aware of it.

If you have not been able or willing to accept God's grace in the matter of your sexuality, here are a few tips for the interim, which I hope you will find helpful:

1. We are told to bring every imagining under submission (cf. II Cor. 10:5). If you find yourself having unwelcome sexual thoughts, ask Jesus for help immediately.

2. Should sexual thoughts come uninvited, don't entertain them. Treat them as unwelcome guests. In other words, command them to leave in the Name of Jesus and then starve them out. Don't allow them a foothold in your life. Sooner or later, they'll leave.

3. Starving implies no feeding. Don't read lurid or even highly romantic books; don't go to see the wrong kinds of movies or knowingly sit through sexy TV shows.

4. Avoid discussing sex unnecessarily. Just the discussion

of it can sometimes stimulate desire.

5. Fill your mind with Scripture. Memorize it; meditate on it. So fill your mind with the Lord that there isn't room for anything else.

6. If falling asleep at night is a problem, put yourself to sleep by reciting Scripture or listening to a good testimony or teaching tape.

7. Always remember that the only real answer is Jesus and complete submission to Him. If you can't completely commit your will to Him in this area, ask Him to bring you to the point where you are willing to do so. He will!

Are we asking God for the impossible when we ask Him for the ability to live a life considered unnatural by the world?

Of course, we are. But our God is a God for whom all things are possible.

"Is anything too hard for the Lord?"

Test Him and see.

Talk about bargains!

Chapter 9

SHOPPING

CENTER

AHEAD

When I was in Israel in 1974, Arab peddlers instantly surrounded my friends and I at each stop, pushing their wares at us.

"Only one dollah," we heard repeated again and again until it became our password for the trip.

"See, Miss, only one dollah for two olivewood ropes of beads."

"Look, look. Color slides, only two dollah and fifty cents."

"Please, lady, lady, buy from me. I give you good deal."

"Hey, Mistah, I give you three camels for your wife." (This was meant as a joke.)

"You want me to sing, 'Jesus Loves Me'? You give me one dollar and I sing. Hallelujah! Praise the Lord!"

"Lady, lady, I give you best bargain anyone can buy."

Obviously the salesman who offered us the "best bargain" was unaware that most of us had already purchased the best bargain anyone can buy. I am, of course, talking about a bargain that can't be bought with money, the bargain you make with God when you accept Jesus Christ as

Savior and Lord. On that day you give Him your tired, soiled, messed-up life in exchange for His Salvation and His new, joyful, clean, fresh life.

The Christian walk involves a whole series of exchanges or convenants with God, trades in which God promises a blessing to those who will obey certain commandments.

Let's look at a covenant God made with the Israelites of the Old Testament which many spiritual Israelites are finding relevant and are claiming for today.

> "If my people, who are called by my name, shall humble themselves and pray, and seek my face and turn from their wicked ways then I will hear from heaven, and will forgive their sin and will heal their land." (II Chron. 7:14)

The next time any of us Christians feels the urge to blame politicians, Communists or the Mafia for the situation that exists in this country, we need to remember God's promise that if *the Christians* will shape up, He will heal our land.

One of the nicer aspects of exchanging with God is that we always come out with the better end of the bargain. Actually, we have nothing to give God (everything is His already) except ourselves. Why God should ever want depraved, selfish, proud, deceitful women and men is a riddle only He can answer. But want us He does and He is willing to trade us some very beautiful and wonderful treasures as we give Him more and more of ourselves.

A search through your Bible can utterly astound you if you are not already aware that the entire Bible is underlaid with this exchange principle:

> "Ask and it shall be given you;
> Seek and ye shall find;
> Knock and it shall be opened unto you;
> For everyone that asketh receiveth, and he that seeketh findeth; and to him that knocketh it shall be opened." (Matt. 7:7-8)

Most of us are where we are today in our Christian walk because we have or have not tested the validity of God's promises and engaged in a series of exchanges with Him.

I believe these exchange promises should have special

meaning for women in general because women, by nature, are more inclined to recognize their incompleteness without God. This applies in an even greater degree to single women, who are probably acutely, even painfully, aware of the emptiness of a life without the Lord.

Both immediately before and after my marriage ended, I desperately sought the Lord and He truly rewarded my seeking, first with a revelation of Himself as Savior and Lord, later as the Baptizer in the Holy Spirit, and now as Father and Teacher, the One who purifies and prepares me for my place in the Body of Christ.

Many of the exchanges God offers are easy to recognize, but let's look at some of the Scripture you may not have considered as featuring exchanges. The sixty-first chapter of Isaiah is particularly rich in this aspect.

> "The Spirit of the Lord God is upon me because the Lord hath anointed me to preach good tidings unto the meek; he hath sent me to bind up the brokenhearted, to proclaim liberty to the captives, and the opening of the prison to those who are bound.
> "To proclaim the acceptable year of the Lord and the day of vengeance of our God, to comfort all that mourn;
> "To appoint unto those who mourn in Zion, to give unto them beauty for ashes, the oil of joy for mourning, the garment of praise for the spirit of heaviness that they might be called trees of righteousness, the planting of the Lord, that he might be glorified." (Isa. 61:1-3)

There are enough offers of exchanges in these verses to carry us through most of the trials of a lifetime.

Look at Verse 3, where the exchanges are so plainly laid out:

First, the Lord stands willing and able to give us beauty, but He wants something for that beauty, the ashes of our lives. Ashes in the natural are what remain after fire has done its job. We Christians have a fire in our lives, the fire of the Holy Spirit, and it is the Holy Spirit's job to burn away the dross: *our* dreams, *our* desires, *our* purposes, *our* works.

The ashes that remain are waste. They can't do any good

and they may "clog up" our lives. They are meant to be disposed of. God is not only willing to take them away; He'll replace them with beauty.

The second exchange the Lord is eager to make with us in this verse is to give us the oil of joy, if we will first give Him our mourning. Mourning can be described as the residue after death has removed *our* dreams, *our* desires, *our* purposes, *our* works.

I know a woman who, after losing her husband, has tried to fill her emptiness with mourning. "Of course, I grieve for Ed," she explains to friends. "I would feel disloyal to his memory if I didn't. I'll mourn for him until I die."

Her way is a very poor way of filling the emptiness of life. God has a better way. We give Him our mourning; He gives us joy!

Finally, the Lord wants to trade us our spirit of heaviness for the garment of praise. The spirit of heaviness can be a real depression or merely the "blahs" we experience. It can be worry or just fretting on our part. Whatever it is, it's difficult to shake on our own, as is evidenced by the number of people who seek psychiatric help or even attempt suicide each year, merely because of something called depression.

God's remedy for this heaviness is praise. Yes, praise whether we feel like praising or not! The times when we don't feel like praising the Lord, we can offer Him a sacrifice of praise. And, believe me, in the beginning it may very well be a sacrifice. But if we will continue to praise Him He will give us the *garment* of praise; we will be literally clothed and covered with praises for Him.

Now, for a minute, let's take a look at God's side of these exchanges. Just what does the Lord get out of all this trading? The third verse explains this too, "that we might be called trees of righteousness—the planting of the Lord that He might be glorified."

The Lord wants glory; yet even glorifying the Lord is for our benefit, too. We are made so that our lives come into

104

proper perspective only when we recognize Who the Lord is and glorify Him for it.

All these exchanges and many more are implicit in the greatest exchange of all—Salvation. It will take us a lifetime and into eternity to understand everything we received when we accepted Salvation, but let's look at some of its implications in Verses 1 and 2 of Isaiah 61.

" . . . The Lord has anointed me to bring good news to the suffering and afflicted . . . " Are you hurt or afflicted in any way?

" . . . he has sent me to comfort the brokenhearted . . ." Is your heart broken? Are bitter memories keeping the break infected?

" . . . to announce liberty to the captives . . ." You are captive to whatever keeps you from full participation in the Lord's blessings.

" . . . to open the eyes of the blind . . ." Any area of your life that is not filled with the light of Jesus is a blind area.

" . . . to those who mourn that the time of God's favor to them has come . . ." What do you regret? What are you grieving over—lost opportunities, your youth, your mistakes?

Salvation in its fullness is the remedy to all these problems. The Good News is that God will heal us physically, mentally and spiritually, erase old memories, free us from all that binds, open the eyes of our understanding and crown us with God's favor—He will do all this and more—in exchange for our commitment.

Does it sound too glib, too easy? Is there a catch somewhere? Yes, in a way there is. And this is the catch. *An offer to exchange is worthless if we don't actually make the exchange.*

One year, following Christmas, a local store offered to exchange Christmas presents anyone received from any store but didn't like, for something of equal value from its stock.

Now it happened that that Christmas I had received a blouse I absolutely hated. The store's offer really intrigued me, but unfortunately, I never got around to taking the blouse to the store. Every time I looked in my closet during the next year, there was that ugly blouse, Knowing I could have done something about it and hadn't made me feel that much worse.

The next year when the store made the same offer I was there on the first day to exchange my blouse for a much prettier one.

Perhaps you feel that you have sincerely tried to make these exchanges with the Lord, but somehow the trade has never been completed. What can you do then? If this is your situation, I believe you should pray for the Holy Spirit to give you insight into your unconscious motives.

The Lord did this for me one day at school when I felt myself coming down with a "bug."

As I prayed for healing the Lord spoke to me, "Do you want to be healed so much that you will never again compare sicknesses with your friends?"

I knew exactly what He meant. In our society, "I can be sicker than you," and "My symptoms are more interesting than your symptoms," are favorite games many of us play with a fervor.

I was candidly honest. "Of course not," I said in answer to the Lord's question.

I don't know whether the Lord respected my honesty or not. I do know I didn't get healed that day, but I did begin to understand why I sometimes had not received healing on other occasions.

If you see yourself in my examples, if you have not yet discovered that the Lord is offering you something more and better than bitterness against an ex-husband or a family, if there is someone in your life you think you can never forgive, if you have ugly memories you can't forget, if you feel you would have little to talk about if you stopped discussing your symptoms or that no one would pay any attention to you if you didn't have so many problems, then take these things to the Lord right now, express your sorrow for them and pray that the Lord will quickly make you ready to exchange your problems for what He is offering.

"For God has planted them like strong and graceful oaks for His own glory." (Isa. 61:3b TLB)

Let our joy, our freedom shine forth for the glory of the Lord.

**"This is the day the Lord has made.
We will rejoice and be glad in it."**

Chapter 10

PEDESTRIANS

ONLY

Four of us teachers were discussing some extremely troubled teen-agers. The entire gist of the conversation was negative. No one saw much hope for these kids at all. Finally one teacher turned to me and asked, "What do you think the answer is, Jo Anne?"

It isn't often that someone asks me such a leading question. I gulped, then said quietly, "I think the only answer is Jesus. I don't think these kids have a chance or a future without Him."

I'll never forget the startled look on that teacher's face. "Do you mean you think God is really concerned with someone's everyday life?" he asked incredulously.

In thinking over the conversation later, I realized that his shock was based on the fact that he had never considered a God who loves His creatures and wants to become involved in their personal lives. A non-Christian, he had ideas about Christianity that were of the "pie-in-the-sky" variety: a person became a Christian so he would have a guarantee of getting to heaven someday or as some wags have called it his "fire insurance."

Unfortunately, there are too many people, even those bearing the name Christian, who have never gotten much further in their thinking than my teacher friend. They expect to meet God in heaven someday, but in the meantime they're strictly on their own. Any idea of a personal relationship with a God vitally interested in the day-to-day affairs of man is too far out to consider.

True, the Bible is a book about a glorious future. But, primarily, I believe it is a book about the glorious present.

"This is the day which the Lord hath made; we will rejoice and be glad in it." (Ps. 118:24)

"So do not worry or be anxious about tomorrow." (Matt. 6:34 Amp.)

"Now faith is . . ." (Heb. 11:1)

Possibly, just possibly, the best part of the Good News is that God gives us the wherewithal to live today joyously, no matter what our circumstances are. If present-day Christianity has made no other contribution its rediscovery and emphasis that our faith is for today, rather than some wonderful day in the future, has justified its existence.

All of us travel with a lot of excess baggage. Part of my excess baggage was an advanced case of self-pity. One of the neatest things the Lord ever did for me after Salvation and the Baptism in the Holy Spirit was to take the self-pity away.

Self-pity or over-concern about our present or future status is the biggest burden anyone can carry with her. I know this from personal experience. I certainly carried that weight around long enough.

Oh, how I used to shed tears worrying about my future, fretting over why I had to be one to go it alone, feeling lonely and sorry for myself.

But, praise the Lord, Jesus took away that self-pity and made me feel capable and competent in Him. Now, when a problem or a situation seems more than I can handle or bear,

I am learning to rest in Him and wait for the blessing to come.

I believe that every problem is accompanied by a blessing. Doesn't the Bible promise, "There hath no temptation taken you, but such is common to man, but God is faithful, who will not suffer you to be tempted above that ye are able, but will, with the temptation, also make a way to escape, that ye may be able to bear it."? (I Cor. 10:13)

This is the day the Lord has made—today—this very day and He has put or allowed you to be placed exactly where you are in your precise condition.

Also, I believe that if your condition is undesirable to you, your best chance of getting out of it is to triumph over it rather than surrender to it.

Teachers have a cliche that is frequently recited as a joke but, nevertheless, has a lot of truth to it: "There are no problems, only challenges."

If you are unhappy, let your situation be a challenge to you. Let God's wisdom, not your own, supply the solution. Pray and ask for guidance, then relax, quit worrying and see what the Lord shows you to do about overcoming the situation.

The Golden Rule is so important in friendship. If you lack friends, learn how to be a friend. If social life is important to you and no one invites you anywhere, you start inviting people.

Seek fellowship. There are so many women in our shoes today that none of us need ever be lonely. We need to get together, share together, pray together and socialize together. One of the most rewarding prayer groups I was ever in was one composed of single people only. We could pray together because we shared many of the same problems; we knew what it meant to walk in one another's shoes.

We also need to widen our circle of friends and this should include married people as well as single.

Do you want peace of mind? Then accept your singleness, at least for the time being. "But isn't there someone for me?"

you ask. Yes, there is Someone and His Name is Jesus, and if you will let Him, He is sufficient for you.

Why not commit your singleness to Him?

Paul had a lot to say about the advantages of the single state: "For I would that all men were even as I myself am [satisfied with the single life]. But every man hath his proper gift of God, one after this manner and another after that. I say, therefore, to the unmarried and widows, it is good for them if they abide as I." (I Cor. 7:7,8)

He had more to say in Verse 34. "The unmarried woman careth for the things of the Lord, that she may be holy in body and in spirit, but she that is married careth for the things of the world, how she may please her husband."

For too long now a great portion of the Church has passed Paul's words off as the advice of a crotchety old bachelor without weighing the wisdom of his comments.

The Catholic Church has long honored the single state by providing for nuns and priests in their life-long vocation. I believe the time is already here when God is leading some men and women from all denominations into a life of singleness dedicated to Him, as definitely as He is leading others into a life of marriage. But, whereas in past ages, these dedicated singles were set apart in religious communities, today they may very well live and function within the course of everyday life.

I am not trying to glorify the single state. I am merely saying that, dedicated to God, it is an honorable one and one I urge you to at least consider as you seek the Lord's will for your life. It certainly has many advantages and it is a rare married woman who does not occasionally cast covetous eyes in your direction when her responsibilities limit her activities, or her marriage is less than perfect. I have one married friend who still thinks my single life is the greatest one possible.

Granted, singleness does come with its built-in problems, but so does marriage.

If you are a woman who knows in her heart that she can

never be completely satisfied without marriage you may wonder what the future holds for you in light of scriptural guidance.

If you are a never-been-married girl, you have the choice, of course, of staying single or of marrying. Neither state is superior in itself. The only important question is: what is God's will for your life? However, as a Christian, should you marry, you are obligated to marry a Christian. "Be ye not unequally yoked together with unbelievers; for what fellowship hath righteousness with unrighteousness?" (II Cor. 6:14)

In this day and age when one-third to one-half of all marriages will be dissolved, it is a source of wonder how any marriage that is not Christian has a chance of surviving. One recent survey has indicated that one-half of all marriages (in which one or both parties are not Christians) end in divorce, but where both parties are practicing Christians, only one in 1084 will end in divorce. The odds show the difference Jesus makes in a marriage.

If you agree that you will marry only a Christian, then you are wasting your time in even dating non-Christians. What's probably worse is that you may be playing with fire, because the possibility that you will fall in love with one of the non-Christians you are dating is very real.

Don't kid yourself that if you begin to "get serious" you will break off with that person. The "flesh" doesn't work that way. I always feel sad when I see the Christian children of an "unequal yoking," who from their own experience should know the problems that develop in such a union, nevertheless repeat the mistake of marrying a non-Christian. A few years later, when they are older or have children, their need for Jesus grows and they find themselves in exactly the same position as their Christian parent was.

According to the Bible, the widow is free to marry or not marry as she sees fit; however, Paul actually encouraged young widows to remarry.

The avenues open for the divorced woman are just not that

clear cut. Those who contend that the divorcee should be allowed to remarry as long as she marries a Christian say that refusal on the part of the Church to let her marry means that the Body of Christ is holding up divorce as the one sin God cannot forgive. Or, they cite Gen. 2:18: "It is not good that the man should be alone," or I Cor. 7:9, "But if they cannot have self-control, let them marry; for it is better to marry than to burn." (Scofield)

Still others insist that if she has been left by a non-Christian husband she is free to remarry, basing their belief on I Corinthians, "But if the unbelieving depart, let him depart. A brother or a sister is not under bondage in such cases . . ." (Chapter 7, Verse 15)

The Catholic Church has long held that some so-called marriages are not valid and, for a variety of reasons, has granted annulments which say, in effect, that the marriage never took place and thus the person is free to marry.

Still other groups believe that unless a marriage is dissolved by death it remains in force in God's eyes, no matter what legal steps are taken on earth.

I would be remiss if I tried to influence others with my personal convictions on such a controversial subject. But I do urge you to discover for yourself God's will in your own life on this matter. I also urge you to follow the teachings of your particular church or denomination. Do it before you are faced with the problem of remarriage. After you have fallen in love is no time to figure out what you really believe. At that point such an effort is usually worthless because you are too likely to follow only your own feelings and inclinations.

Should you decide that it is right to remarry, let God pick your next husband. Too many of us botched it up when we tried to pick "Mr. Right" on our own.

On the other hand, should you come to the conclusion that you are not to remarry, then why court temptation by dating? Truly accept your role as the "wife of Christ" and let Him be the only important man in your life.

No matter why you are single at this time in your life, why not give "these best years" to the Lord's service? Relax in the knowledge that He will then guide your paths and let you know whether He will have you continue in your singleness or join you in a Christian marriage some day. He will work out what is best for you in His perfect timing.

Then you can truly begin each morning's journey with the knowledge that, "This is the day which the Lord hath made." And rejoice in it!

Chapter 11

SCHOOL

CROSSING

It is common in some Christian circles to hear the question, "How well do you know the Lord?"

Let me ask you the other side of the question: "How well do you think the Lord knows *you?*"

The success of your single walk (whether temporary or permanent) may very well be determined by your answer.

How well does the Lord know any of us?

David had very definite thoughts on that subject, recorded in Psalm 139, "You made all the delicate inner parts of my body and knit them together in my mother's womb." (Verse 13 TLB)

"Oh, Lord, you have examined my heart and know everything about me. You know when I sit or stand. When far away you know my every thought . . . every moment, you know where I am. You know what I am going to say before I even say it . . ." (Verses 1-4 TLB)

"How precious it is, Lord, to realize that you are thinking about me constantly! I can't even count how many times a day your thoughts turn toward me. And when I waken in the morning, you are still thinking of me." (Verses 17-18 TLB)

The Psalmist tells us that the Lord knew us before we were even born. He knows our every thought, our every action and He is thinking of us constantly. To which Jesus added that even "the very hairs of your head are all numbered." (Matt. 10:30 TLB)

How's that for starters?

Equally important is knowing how well God knows us is how He feels about us.

Let's start with some of the most familiar Scriptures:

"For God so loved the world that He gave His only begotten Son that whosoever believeth in Him should not perish but have everlasting life." (John 3:16)

"We love Him, because He first loved us." (I John 4:19)

"For I am persuaded that neither death nor life, nor angels, nor principalities, nor powers, nor things present, nor things to come, nor height, nor depth, nor any other creatures, shall be able to separate us from the love of God, which is in Christ Jesus, our Lord." (Rom. 8:38-39)

"Herein is love, not that we loved God, but that He loved us and sent His Son to be the propitiation for our sins." (I John 4:10)

The picture the Bible gives us of God is a far different one than some people would have us see. Too many times we have been presented with theories of a creative power or of a cold, impersonal God who, though He created man, is certainly not interested in him as an individual, or concerned with our petty little problems, our needs, our destinies.

I remember, when I was a college student, being told by an older woman acquaintance that my idea of a "personal" God was cute but immature, the implication being that when I grew up a little, I would see how silly the whole idea was. I didn't argue with her, but I remember my sense of outrage at her idea of God. Maybe I was selfish; maybe I was immature, but what good to me was a God who didn't care about me?

Actually as I grew older, I found I needed a "personal" God more than ever.

Thank God, we do have a God who cares for us, who is intimately involved with us every minute of the day and night. He loves us so much that when Adam and Eve (and every man and woman since then, with the exception of Jesus and possibly Enoch) blew the chance of spending eternity with Him, He still wanted us so much that He decided to pay the price Himself that a second chance for us cost.

How's that for love?

This love of God for us is something we human beings will probably never fully understand, but God created us for His pleasure—that means *we give Him pleasure.* Although the Bible declares this idea I had never really given it much thought till recently. I guess I always more or less pictured God sitting in heaven, wringing His hands and crying over us and our mistakes, and wondering if we really were worth all the trouble and heartache. Then one evening the Lord showed me a different picture through an incident at home.

We're cat lovers in my family and the present feline population in the house is three, plus one dog. Admittedly, all the animals are badly spoiled and I get most of my exercise just opening the door so they can go in and out.

One evening while trying to read I was first interrupted by the dog wanting out. I had no sooner sat down than the cat wanted in. Next the dog wanted back in the house. Again, I sat down just in time to see another cat scurry to the door.

As I let her out I complained, "Oh, you animals, you're a pain." Then I thought of how much I enjoyed them and I added, "But I guess you're worth it."

The minute I said that, God spoke in my heart. "That's the way I feel about My children," He said. "I delight in them."

Later, reading my Berkeley translation of the Bible, I found a similar use of words. Matthew 3:17 says, "And a voice from heaven said, 'This is My Son, the Beloved, in whom I delight.' "

His words made me weep. To think of how much trouble we cause the Lord, how weary we must make Him with all our moanings and complainings and misunderstandings. And still He delights in everyone of us who are His children!

How like a true father! How like the picture of the father shown in the story of the prodigal son. We love that picture of fatherhood, don't we, even if we don't quite understand the concept. It's the one we're most fond of—the patient Father who loves us so much He's always willing to forgive us.

However, there's another side of fatherhood we aren't always so eager to accept. This is the side which causes a parent to train up a child in the way he wants him to go—a parent who restricts, withholds, disciplines and even punishes. But this side of fatherhood or parenthood is just as important as the other. Few children would survive without such schooling.

I think of my own children; when they were little, discipline was terribly important. I couldn't let them play in the street if I believed it was dangerous, no matter how much they begged and carried on.

When they broke the rules I had laid down, they had to be punished, even if every other child in the neighborhood got away with the same thing.

Now that they are older, I try to teach them to discipline themselves—work before play, get enough sleep, say "no" to your friends when they encourage you to do something wrong. However, if they won't discipline themselves, I must do it for them. I will set the working hours, the sleeping hours, the limits.

This is a big part of being a parent but not necessarily the most pleasant part. I believe that this is a big part of God's role as our Father, too.

I can't help sometimes wondering what happened after the prodigal son returned home. There were bound to be problems—this was still the same son who had left home and squandered his inheritance. Even though he was sorry, he probably still had a lot of learning to do before he became the son his father wanted.

I imagine there were times when he wasn't as humble as he was when he first returned. I imagine there were times when his father still had to be firm, lay down the law, and perhaps even punish him.

When God as our Father decides it's time for His child to move, to change, to grow, He has a few advantages over a human parent. As a human parent, I can only imperfectly love my children, imperfectly know what they are doing at all times, and imperfectly discipline them and direct them towards their goals.

With God, it is a different story!

He perfectly loves us.

He is omnipresent (everywhere).

He has perfect knowledge.

Isn't it only logical that He is the one to trust with every area of our life?

I said every area.

Yes, even our singleness!

Oh, I know how difficult that is for a woman to do. I fought the Lord on this for so many years. I was willing to give Him nearly all aspects of my life—"but not my singleness, Lord!"

I can only describe the reason behind my refusal as a lack of trust, a sort of "You know what God's really like; if I give Him my singleness, He'll keep me single," attitude.

I can't say that it was increased trust that finally led to my surrender; it was my absolute dissatisfaction with my handling of my single state. So one night at a meeting when the speaker encouraged everyone there to give Jesus any area which he or she was holding back, I reluctantly gave Him my single status to do with whatever He chose, including the right to keep me single.

It was almost that simple. He took it and has never given it back, nor have I seriously tried to take it back. It was one of the best exchanges I have ever made. In return the Lord has given me a contentment, a comfortableness, a joy in being single that I never previously enjoyed. I am content now to let the Lord choose my marital state (or lack of it), knowing that He will work through the one that will develop those characteristics He wants developed in me.

The only thing I regret about the whole transaction is that I waited so long. Just think, the Lord could have done this for me years ago, if I had only let Him. He's anxious to do the same for anyone else.

You may recall that I said earlier that the Lord can work only with those things we give Him. You see, the Lord has to work with my present condition, even though it may not be the one He wanted for me had I been in His perfect will many years ago. Someday, He may even change my situation, but I am confident that before He will change it He has some more changing to do in me. Meanwhile I'm content to trust Him, and just pray that I'll cooperate with Him in all things.

Oh, how we struggle sometimes when the Lord tries to do something in us, even something that's for our own good.

My friend Sharon was reminded of this one day recently when she ran outdoors to rescue her kitten from a pack of dogs. Picking up the kitten, Sharon was rewarded with several bad scratches.

"I'm trying to save your life, Dummy," Sharon scolded the kitten, "and look at how you act."

The kitten did not reply, but the Lord did. "That's exactly the way you behave when I try to do something for your own good," He said. Sharon, who is usually quite talkative, didn't have anything to say.

How do you act when the Lord tries to do something in your life? He is trying to do something very important right now that *He can do best through your being single.*

Will you let him?

Won't you this very minute offer your singleness to Him,

whether you are alone through choice or not, whether you are divorced, widowed or never married?

Then sit back and let Him who travels with you at all times work in your life.

**I don't have much to say, Lord,
except it's so good to be with You.**

Chapter 12

WELCOME

HOME

May I ask you a question?

"How would you like to be married to a husband who is always faithful, ever concerned for your welfare, who wants only the best for you and who will love you no matter what you do?

In case that question was too easily answered, let me ask you another one.

"Do you take your Bible literally?"

Just to be difficult, I'm going to be persistent.

"Are you sure?"

I believe most Christian women at this point would answer most emphatically, "Of course, I'm sure."

Well, then, if we're really so sure, let's try this bit of Scripture on for size: "For thy Maker is thine husband; the Lord of hosts is his name and thy Redeemer, the Holy One of Israel, the God of the whole earth shall he be called." (Isa. 54:5)

Surprise! The Bible says we already have exactly that kind

of husband.

The God of the Universe my husband! What a mind-blowing idea.

Well, that's what God has said, and I think He not only means what He says, but that He means it very literally. I think He's been waiting a long time for those unmarried women to come to that point in their journey where they will take Him seriously. I think He wants to prove His promises to us.

Well, what's stopping Him then? Let's consider at least one possibility.

One morning while I was praying I reminded the Lord that I was His wife and as a wife I was doing a lot of things I didn't think it was a wife's place to do. I told Him I thought that, as my Husband, He should be doing them.

As quickly as I got the words out of my mouth the Lord answered, "Then why don't you let Me do them?"

You know His words really stopped me short, for two very important reasons: First and foremost, I had to question them as you must question any voices and thoughts: "Was that really God speaking to me?" My spirit assured me that it was indeed the Lord who had spoken.

That brought me face to face with the second reason. With a sinking feeling I realized that though I might complain and "mutter" to the Lord, I really wasn't that ready to trust Him completely in the role of husband.

The test issue at stake right then was my daughter's car (car problems loom large in a single woman's life). The car wasn't operating well and trying to find the source of the trouble was causing me a lot of lost time and tension.

Now the Lord was taking me at my word (actually, it was at His Word) so it was all up to me. I could either put up or shut up. That being the case, what was the next step?

For once, I decided to play it smart. If the Lord really wanted me to be His wife, let Him prove His sincerity. I determined I would not make another move toward getting the car fixed. If that meant the car would sit in front of the house for the next month, then sit it would. That car was in the Lord's hands.

Immediately, I had a sense of peace about the whole situation.

Before I could do anything (especially nothing) the Lord opened the "eyes of my understanding" a little. In effect, He showed me how wrong I had been all along in taking the responsibility for that car's operation. The car was my daughter's problem. She had to assume responsibility for it. I was, in fact, playing the role of the over-protective mother.

It took Les a couple days to get moving, but once she learned I would not lend her my car except for emergencies she found someone to fix her car. About an hour's work and that car was running.

While we're on the subject of children, let me add that I believe that as our husband, the Lord also wants to be the father of our children in the real sense of the word.

A divorced friend, Patty, frequently went to the Lord about her concerns for her five children. She was finding it more and more difficult to be both father and mother to them. One day while she was praying the Lord spoke to her heart. "Stop trying to be a father to them," He said. "I'm their Father."

Patty has taken the Lord at His Word, and so thoroughly has she convinced her children that they have a Heavenly Father watching over them that recently when she had to leave them for a weekend she reminded them that while she could not necessarily know if they did anything they shouldn't, their Heavenly Father could certainly see everything they did. To which reminder, her youngest son exclaimed, "That's not fair."

Needless to say, no one got in trouble that weekend.

It seems to be a quirk of human nature that we so frequently will trust the Lord only after we have run out of our own human resources. Fortunately for me, I ran out of human resources very early in the game when it came to home repairs, and I have had to trust the Lord to keep my house from falling down around my ears. He has furnished me with a series of people who could do the repairs as I had needs that I brought to Him. Sometimes I paid for their labors; other times, when I didn't have the money, I didn't have to. I have also learned to do some things for myself.

Interestingly enough, the Lord used non-Christians to help me almost all the time. It is a never-ending source of amazement to me how non-Christians frequently have more empathy for our problems than do Christians. I do not mean to say this critically because I, as often as anyone (probably more often), have been put to shame by the love and generosity of non-Christians.

Another area in which the Lord has dealt with me, is that if He is to be Husband to me, then I must be a wife to Him.

First of all, a husband is usually delighted with a wife who seeks him out just for his company. The truly faithful and loving wife will want to fellowship with her husband and to minister to him. If he is away, she will read and reread his love letters and will remember everything he has ever said to her.

Fortunately, the Lord is not like many husbands who are more interested in their football game viewing than in sharing time with their wives, or who are better at doing things *for* their wives than in *being with them*.

We, who have a Heavenly Husband, are so blessed because we need only seek Him out and He is there, ready and willing to fellowship. His love for us and desire to be with us is unaffected by mood, climate, the latest stock reports or how the boss reacted to his most recent suggestion.

A single woman friend of mine related how one evening she was filled with a strange restlessness. She tried working, she tried reading, all to no avail. The restlessness persisted. Finally she cried out, "What is it, Lord? What do You want?"

"I just want to be with you," the Lord answered.

Then followed two of the most glorious hours of

fellowshipping with the Lord she had ever spent.

Another area in which we are called to act like wives is in praising our Husband, both to His face and to others as well. Every husband likes a wife who thinks he is wonderful and in the Lord's case He is absolutely worthy of our praise. Because our relationship with the Lord is basically a love one, we should spend much of our time with Him just telling Him how wonderful He is and how much we love Him. We must also remember to thank Him for all He's done and is doing for us.

No husband is pleased when his wife nags and complains. In the Bible such complaining against God is called murmuring and it is very clear that it is displeasing to the Lord. Paul warned in I Corinthians "And don't murmur against God and His dealings with you, as some of them did, for that is why God sent His Angel to destroy them. All of these things happened to them as examples—as object lessons to us—to warn us against doing the same things; they were written down so that we could read about them and learn from them in these last days as the world nears its end." (I Cor. 10:10,11 TLB)

Apparently, the Lord feels very strongly against the so-called murmuring most of us indulge in. Despite a warning like this, how many of us spend a good deal of time complaining to the Lord about how He has treated us, fussing about what He has or has not done?

In our relationships with others, who are we more likely to do things for—the person who thanks us from his heart or the one for whom we can never do enough, and who obviously feels we owe him more than he is getting? The former, for sure.

I feel that God is not basically any different. I believe He gives His gifts in abundance to those who truly have grateful hearts.

Next, I believe that the Lord not only wants us to be wives to Him, but that He expects us to be faithful wives. This means that we cannot indulge in any compromising situations

129

any more than any other wife can.

If we are depending on the Lord to take care of our home repairs or to find companionship for us, for example, then He will not send us help or friendships with strings attached.

Lillian, a widow, found a retired handyman to come in and take care of her plumbing problems very inexpensively. She was delighted with his work—that is, until he began telephoning her about once a week. The calls seemed harmless enough, and yet he always managed to bring the subject around to the fact that his wife was out for the evening and that he was lonely.

Another single woman thought she had found the answer to inexpensive car repairs when her neighbor, with his wife's consent, said to call on him any time she needed help. She did call on him a couple of times, but she quickly became aware that this gentleman, completely circumspect on any other occasion, always managed to bring the conversation around to sex whenever they were alone. Nancy did not need a counselor's advice to tell her that this man's help did not come from the Lord.

In case you missed my point, sisters dear, both of these offers of help came with strings attached, and if consoling a lonesome husband or discussing sexual relations is the price you are expected to pay for this help, then it is out of your price range. Your Husband wouldn't like it.

When Lynn was first divorced, a very good friend frequently invited her daughters and her over to spend the day or a weekend. She was truly grateful for the hospitality; a family in her position didn't receive many invitations from families.

All went well and even the husband seemed genuinely glad to see them. Then one afternoon when the husband and Lynn momentarily happened to be alone in the house, he made a grab for her.

Lynn does not know to this day if he lunged at every woman with whom he found himself alone, or whether she looked willing or just what the problem was. But as much as she loved and appreciated her friend and no matter how lonely she was, she knew she could accept no more invitations to her home.

Finally, I think the Lord is looking for a wife who will be submissive and obedient to Him. When I speak of obedience here, I mean a discerning of His perfect will for us personally, rather than His permissive will. We all know mortal husbands who, after much nagging, give in to their wives or permit them to do something because they so obviously want to do it, even when it goes against the husband's feelings.

The Lord is sometimes like that. If we fuss enough He will sometimes permit us to go our own ways but, oh, how much He would rather have us do as He wishes and what He knows is best for us.

The Lord gave me a painful illustration of this. One day after a series of episodes I was "discussing" my older daughter with Him. She was a good girl, probably more obedient than many children. But on the other hand she had a way of getting me to allow her to do things I didn't always think were best for her, just because she would beg so hard or else because doing them seemed so important to her.

I was more or less using the Lord for the moment as a sounding board to sort out my feelings about my daughter, and finally, with a burst of insight, I said, "It's not that she's disobedient, Lord; it's just that she isn't interested in learning what I really would like her to do. She'd much rather try to get me to go along with *her* wishes."

"But that's the way *you* are," the Lord said.

This was easily the most painful revelation of myself the Lord has ever given me. His words so physically pained me, as I recognized their truth, that I burst into tears.

How well the Lord knew me. By nature I was rather legalistic and I usually tried to be obedient to His commands as they are written in the Bible. All too frequently, however, I had resisted learning His specific desires for me in every area

131

of my life and being obedient to those desires.

When a man and a woman are married in our culture we say that the woman "takes" her husband's name. If at some later date she does not live up to her marriage vows, she has in a very real sense taken her husband's name in vain.

We who are called by the Lord's Name might do well to remember that taking His Name in vain is a sin.

"For thy Maker is thy husband . . ."

Let us learn to truly be the kind of wife God desires.

Wow! The Lord sure provides in a big way!

EPILOGUE

Once several years ago after my mother first contracted leukemia and by all rights should have died (but didn't) and after my older daughter was hit and thrown by a car and should have been killed (but wasn't) the Lord told me, "See, I told you I would never leave you an orphan."

"Oh, Lord," I laughed, "that isn't what that Scripture means."

"It's My Book," the Lord corrected me. "It means whatever I say it means."

The passing years have taught me the truth of the Lord's words on many different levels.

Perhaps it is no coincidence that during these past days, as I have struggled to finish this book, my life has been turned upside down, physically and emotionally. Tonight, I, who have dreaded the day when I would be alone, am really alone for the first time in my life.

But I am *not* alone! Truly He has not left me an orphan. All around me I feel the love and concern of my real family, the Body of Christ. And He is here, my Father, my Husband, my Lord and Savior, my Comforter, filling me with the peace only He can give, flooding me with His incredible joy that only He has to offer.

So at this rest spot in the middle of a very dry land, I have drunk deeply. And though I have fasted, I have eaten my fill at the Lord's table. This seeming desert is in reality an oasis, and the Lord has exchanged my dried out sack lunch for a banquet.

The banquet is for you, too, my sisters; it is for you.

The invitation has been extended. The feast is prepared. The Lord of the banquet awaits you. Won't you come and dine?

Your sister in Christ,
Jo Anne Sekowsky
Summer, 1974

Aglow Bible Studies

Wouldn't you like to start an Aglow Bible Study in your neighborhood?

Aglow Bible Studies are written especially for the woman who desires to discover the practical application of the Word of God to her daily life. These studies are designed to be used by the individual woman, the small Bible study group or even a large Bible study group. Each course offers a basic self-guided study approach with optional supplemental material for more intensive study. A new Aglow Bible Study is published each quarter.

NAME _____

ADDRESS _____

CITY _____

STATE _____ ZIP _____

**Order from: Aglow Publications
7715 236th S.W., Edmonds, WA 98020**

Please send me:

____ #1 Creation
____ #2 God's Daughter
____ #3 Fruit of the Spirit
____ #4 Gifts of the Spirit
____ #5 Basic Beliefs
____ #6 Patterns for Parents

$1.50 each
12/$16, 25/$30, 50/$55

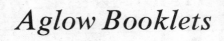

Aglow Booklets

Booklets that will bless you and your friends!

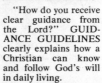

This popular Aglow counseling-witnessing booklet, **RECEIVE ALL GOD HAS TO GIVE**, presents the whole gospel in a simple way. A practical aid for witnessing!

"How do you receive clear guidance from the Lord?" **GUIDANCE GUIDELINES** clearly explains how a Christian can know and follow God's will in daily living.

MY FULL INHERITANCE AS A WOMAN, discusses the relationship of husband and wife as ordained by God, explaining the way to true married love.

NAME _____

ADDRESS _____

CITY _____

STATE _____ ZIP _____

**Order from: Aglow Publications
7715 236th S.W., Edmonds, WA 98020**

Send _____ copies of
RECEIVE ALL GOD
HAS TO GIVE

Send _____ copies of
GUIDANCE GUIDELINES

Send _____ copies of
MY FULL INHERITANCE
AS A WOMAN

50¢ each
2/$1, 10/$4, 25/$8,
50/$15, 100/$25

A Christian Road Map
For Women Traveling Alone

By Jo Anne Sekowsky

$2.50

This is not just another how-to book for single gals. Instead, Jo Anne has chosen to write about the real problems single women face today. In addition, Jo Anne writes for all women who are walking this life alone—physically, emotionally or spiritually. She believes that God does have a special plan for every woman.

Order from your local bookstore or write to:

Aglow Publications
7715 - 236th S.W.
Edmonds, WA 98020

An
Aglow
Best-seller

DATE DUE